# 1917 Halifax Explosion
## and American Response

**Blair Beed**

Dtours Visitors and
Convention Service

Dtours Visitors and Convention Service
PO Box 3443 South
Station Park Lane Centre
Halifax, Nova Scotia, Canada
B3J 3J1
Telephone/Fax: (902) 455-9977

Design: Arthur Carter

Title page photo:
A view of destroyed warehouses in naval Dockyard.

Printed and bound in Nova Scotia by:
McCurdy Printing Limited

Canadian Cataloguing in Publication Data

Beed, Blair, 1955-
1917 Halifax explosion and American response

2nd ed.
ISBN 0-9684383-1-8

1. Halifax (N.S.)—History—Explosion, 1917. 2. Disaster relief—United States—History. I. Dtours Visitors and Convention Service. II. Title.

FC2346.4.B43 1999     971.6'22503     C99-901470-6
F1039.5.H17B43 1999

## DEDICATION

To all those who give aid in times of disaster.

## COVER PHOTO:

Massachucetts State Guard Medical Unit in front of Bellevue, temporary American Hospital, Spring Garden Road, Halifax, December 1917.
From the report of Major Giddings, Massachusetts:
'The morning of December 10 saw the Stars and Stripes flying over the hospital (Bellevue), the first time they had appeared in the city following the disaster. The flag was secured for us by Mr. Ratchesky. It is fitting here to record an incident in connection with the flag. It was brought to our attention that at the Camp Hill Hospital there was a woman from Lowell, Mass., Miss Martha Manter. Captain Harrington, whose home was formerly in Lowell, obtained permission to have Miss Manter transferred to Bellevue. After a good deal of effort the transfer was made. A laundry sleigh was commandeered, as all ambulances were engaged. As the patient was removed from the sleigh and carried into the hospital she broke down and cried. When she finally gained control of herself, Captain Harrington, who thought perhaps the jarring of the sleigh had caused her pain, asked her what was the matter. Her reply was, "The sight of the American flag was too much for me, and I could not control myself. It looked so good to me."'

# CONTENTS

Showing signs of wear, the *Olympic* was a frequent visitor
to Halifax during World War I, with as many as 5,000 war
personnel on board. The recovered bodies from her ill-fated
sister ship *Titanic* had been brought to Halifax in 1912.

# ACKNOWLEDGEMENTS

Many primary sources on the subject of the explosion were consulted. People were most cooperative in helping me to retrieve material and in sharing personal knowledge. Thanks to: State House Archives, Boston; Boston Public Library; Patrick G. Murphy of Halifax and Virginia Cooke of Woonsocket, Rhode Island who assisted me on Boston research; MacDonald School Museum Archives, Middleton, N.S.; Public Library Service, Calgary, Alberta; Leon S. Warmski, Archives of Ontario; Photo Section, City of Toronto Archives; Montreal Public Library; Matthew Rae, Chicago, Illinois. In Halifax, special thanks to Marilyn Gurney, Curator, Maritime Command Museum, Gottingen Street; Sister Mary Martin, Archivist, Mount Saint Vincent Motherhouse Archives; Garry Shutlak and staff of Public Archives of Nova Scotia; Patricia Chalmers, University of King's College Library; Charles Armour, Archivist, Dalhousie University Archives; reference staff, Halifax Regional Library, Spring Garden Road; Janet Kitz; Edith Hartnett; Mary A. Murphy; Violet Dutcher; Janice Coyle, RN; Anna and Alfred Clark; and Trish Flynn.

Photo Credits: Key: L-left, R-right, T-top, M-Middle, B-bottom
Maritime Command Museum: title page, iv, 2, 3B, 11, 14TR, 15, 16, 20, 31, 36R, 47, 49, 53, 64, 68, 70, 71, 77, 78, 89L, 90, 91, 101, 103, 108, 110, 119, 122, 125, 126, 127,129, 131, 133.
Dalhousie University Archives: 39R, 85, 113, 114.
James Collection, City of Toronto Archives: 48.
United Memorial Church/Kitz: 5M, 5B.
Halifax Fire Department Archives: 132.
Mount Saint Vincent Motherhouse Archives: 5T, 41, 88, 92, 96, 97.
Relief Commission Collection, Nathaniel Morse Collection and Notman Collection of the Public Archives of Nova Scotia: cover, 13B, 19, 26T, 81, 87, 116, 122, 128.
Special thanks to survivors and families who allowed me to select from their private collections: viii, ix, x, 1, 3T, 6, 7, 9, 12, 13T, 14TL, 14B, 17,21, 22, 26B, 27, 29, 30, 32, 34, 35, 36L, 37, 38, 39L, 40, 42, 45, 46, 51, 52, 54, 55, 57, 59, 60, 65, 67, 69, 75, 82, 89R, 89T, 89B, 95, 98, 100, 102, 104, 107, 108T, 109, 111, 115, 120, 123, 130, 133.

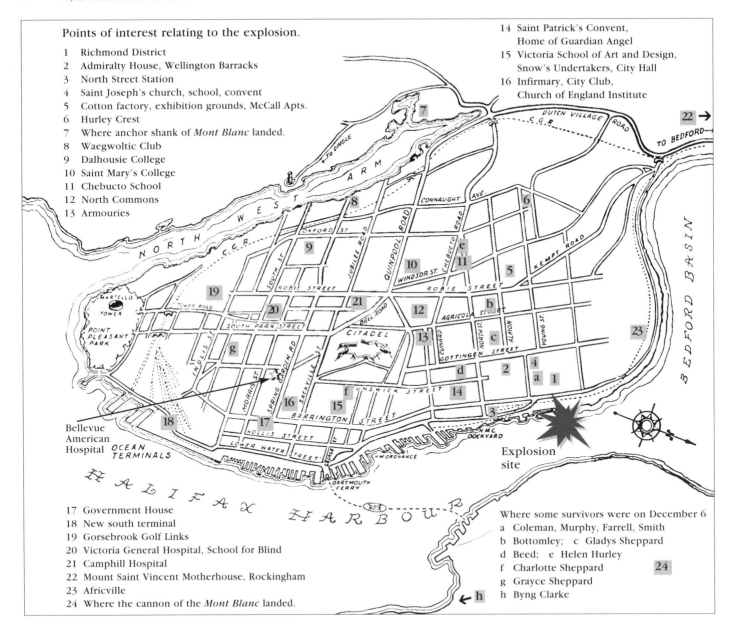

Points of interest relating to the explosion.

1 Richmond District
2 Admiralty House, Wellington Barracks
3 North Street Station
4 Saint Joseph's church, school, convent
5 Cotton factory, exhibition grounds, McCall Apts.
6 Hurley Crest
7 Where anchor shank of *Mont Blanc* landed.
8 Waegwoltic Club
9 Dalhousie College
10 Saint Mary's College
11 Chebucto School
12 North Commons
13 Armouries

14 Saint Patrick's Convent,
   Home of Guardian Angel
15 Victoria School of Art and Design,
   Snow's Undertakers, City Hall
16 Infirmary, City Club,
   Church of England Institute

Bellevue
American
Hospital

Explosion
site

17 Government House
18 New south terminal
19 Gorsebrook Golf Links
20 Victoria General Hospital, School for Blind
21 Camphill Hospital
22 Mount Saint Vincent Motherhouse, Rockingham
23 Africville
24 Where the cannon of the *Mont Blanc* landed.

Where some survivors were on December 6
a  Coleman, Murphy, Farrell, Smith
b  Bottomley;   c  Gladys Sheppard
d  Beed;   e  Helen Hurley
f  Charlotte Sheppard
g  Grayce Sheppard
h  Byng Clarke

# PREFACE

Growing up in Halifax in the 1950s and 1960s, it was still common to see people blinded or disfigured by the Halifax explosion. Every December 6 the newspapers mention the disaster; some anniversary years they include a special supplement. Now as the children of 1917 pass from this life, their obituaries include the words 'survivor of the Halifax Explosion.'

The first stories I learned of the explosion were from my grandmothers, Mary Ann [Mulcahie] Beed and Gladys [Sheppard] Lee. The first event I ever attended relating to the tragedy was *Evening of Music and Words* in 1977 sponsored by the Heritage Trust of Nova Scotia and held at Saint Patrick's Roman Catholic Church on Brunswick Street in Halifax. The church organ provided the sounds of December 6, 1917, the city and the ships in the harbour and then a rumble and the blast; it was a memorable interpretation. After the performance, my aunt Mary [Beed] Gordon, began speaking of her experiences on that fateful day. Each time I have heard a survivor speak of their experiences, I have found it spellbinding. Relatives started my collection of stories of December 6, 1917; friends and neighbours have added to it. Many times in these recollections there has been comments on the generous response from the people of the United States to the needs of the people of Halifax. I incorporate these recollections into my tours and talks and I am rewarded by visitors sharing their stories with me. Some tell of experiences relating directly to the explosion, others, such as people on tour who survived the Texas City disaster or more recent tragedies, identify with the sadness of the 1917 Halifax disaster.

I have kept this book to the style that I use on a tour, something that will make former English teachers cringe. Included are stories from my own collection and letters and diaries written by survivors. I also make reference to newspaper accounts, minutes of the Relief Committee and Commission, the official history of the disaster by Archibald MacMechan, the report of Dr. David Fraser Harris on the Medical Aspects of the Disaster, and files of the State of Massachusetts on the work of the Massachusetts Halifax Relief Committee. In using quotations from original sources spellings and grammar usage have been left as written. Original rounded brackets ( ) are left in place. My comments are in square brackets [ ]. On the basis of research of primary sources I have made corrections to some often repeated 'facts' and to some photograph descriptions. For example, a mistake often repeated '200 children dead in one school' should have been 'over 200 school children dead.' Newspapers of the day printed it incorrectly and some writers have quoted this without referring to original sources. As this is not a research book I have not distracted the reader with footnotes to changes that most would not be aware of. The donation amounts used are mostly listed in Canadian values. At a time when a weekly wage could be $12 a contribution of $1 was a significant amount. Many groups made contributions to relief but I have only noted some to illustrate the variety of offers.

In researching this event I discovered the dead and injured within my own extended family tree of Beed, Mulcahie, Stokes, Hinch, Glenister, Sheppard, Quinn, Hartlin. Over time, through friends' accounts, I have discovered the small town of 1917. Archibald MacMechan, professor and official historian of the disaster, lived across the street from my great grandparents and family, the Sheppard's on Victoria Road. My friends, the Murphy's, lived next door to Vincent Coleman's family on Russell Street. Even now I am still making connection with that past as others share their stories.

I have endeavoured to create a realistic picture of Halifax in 1917-1918. The explosion changed every life in Halifax. This book records the good deeds that came out of the relief effort. The response of the people of the United States in particular has left a lasting impression on the citizens of Halifax. There are other aspects that I have not included. During the recovery of Halifax not everything ran smoothly or fairly. There were people who took advantage of the situation. There were those who took more than they needed and those that charged more than they should have. There were organizational conflicts. In 1918 there were people in charge who felt everyone should be returned to the station of life they had before the disaster. This was fine for those who owned their homes but not for those who rented. There were even

George Street with the Town Clock in the background.

City Hall and Grand Parade dressed for the King's birthday.

cases of people not receiving items or allowances because it was thought 'it might raise their expectations.' There were civic authorities who did not continue with improvements because of 'vested interests.' These aspects of relief are found in *Ground Zero—A Reassessment of the 1917 Explosion in Halifax Harbour* co-edited by Alan Ruffman and Colin D. Howell. Personal stories of other survivors are in *Shattered City* and *Survivors—Children of the Halifax Explosion* by my good friend, Janet Kitz.

Unfortunately for those on a search of buildings that survived the explosion, valuable heritage structures have been lost over the years to poor planning policy. Not enough has been done to mark important sites in Halifax that relate to the largest man made explosion in a populated area before the dropping of the atomic bombs on Japan. Hopefully some readers of this book will take up that challenge.

The Memorial Tower, Halifax, N. S.

Contemporary views of the Memorial Tower on the North-west Arm and the bandstand at the Public Gardens (below).

A pre-explosion view looking south from Cornwallis Street,
towards the downtown business district and the Citadel.

Chapter 1

# HALIFAX BEFORE DECEMBER 6, 1917

*'Halifax sits on her hills by the sea*
*In the might of her pride*
*Invincible terrible beautiful she*
*With a sword at her side'*

Pauline Johnson
Indian Poetess of Canada

A pre World War I composite photo showing British military might in Halifax.

Halifax was founded in 1749 by the British. The town and harbour were fortified against possible invasions. Halifax was port for the North American naval strength of the British Empire which earned it the title 'Warden of the North.'

Princes, privateers and press gangs roamed the streets. Closest mainland port of call to Europe, Halifax would receive news from London and the latest fashions from Paris before the rest of North America.

In the 1800s the city saw the success of local boy, Sir Samuel Cunard, and his steamship line. The age of steam brought ships carrying immigrants for the Canadian West and trains arrived with carloads of goods from elsewhere. Industry puffed away on Nova Scotian coal and profit was still to be made on the military presence.

Halifax's well-to-do expanded their businesses and continued their round of social occasions. The quality of life of the average citizen gradually improved and provision was made for those considered less fortunate. Halifax entered the 1900s proud, prosperous and still ready to serve King and Country.

The twentieth century was a changing world. Oil lamps were still common but gas lights and electric light was used as well. Time saving new inventions were all the rage. An added thrill was having inventors like Marconi and Bell as residents in the province. Halifax was to lose the Royal Navy in 1905 but saw the creation of the Royal Canadian Navy. While Atlantic fishermen were struggling to make a living and many families in Western Canada were living in small huts, the drawing rooms of Halifax sparkled with retained wealth.

Society gathers for Annesley Wedding in 1911 at Saint
Mark's Church of England, Russell Street at Albert Street
in Halifax's Northend.

Above: The Jubilee Boat Club, rowing was a popular pastime of all classes of society.

Right: School for Deaf on Gottingen Street, 92 students were living here in 1917.

In Northend Halifax, the Richmond District, was expanding with new homes and industry. A view looking north to Richmond District, pre 1917. In the foreground Admiralty House can be seen and in the background from left to right rooftops of Russell Street houses, gable and spire of Kaye Street Methodist Church and Wellington Barracks. On the waterfront, overlooking the narrows of Halifax Harbour, smoke billows from the 10 storey Sugar Refinery.

The death of King Edward VII, the sinking of the Titanic in 1912 and the burials of her dead in Halifax were events of interest. In 1913 construction of new ocean terminals in Halifax's Southend was to gain the concerned attention of the Port of Boston. All this was quickly over shadowed by the death of an Archduke and his wife in 1914. Halifax was again at war—'The War to End all Wars.'

Men volunteered and left family and friends for Europe. Sons of the settlers who had settled the West arrived in Halifax bringing wives and families to wait for their safe return from the battlefields of Europe. Others came to work in the war industries. Halifax bustled with cargoes and soldiers for overseas and the city bought its first motorized fire engine, named the Patricia.

Local newspapers gave lists of men killed and wounded on the fields of war. Towns and villages mourned the loss of a generation who had said their last good-byes on Halifax docks. For three years Halifax was involved but still distant from the Great War.

A November 1916 *Halifax Herald* editorial page cartoon reminding people to send gifts to troops overseas.

Left: A Christmas card sent to McKinnon family of Halifax from Sgt. John A. Beed serving in France.

A military town during peace or war can be an exciting place. Some are interested in the ships coming and going. Others watch the passing parade. As a boy on Russell Street, Walter Murphy had a front row view of military men going to the neighbourhood churches and later wrote of it for his church bulletin:

## Memories of a Parishioner over Forty
### by Walter Murphy

'The drum I got at the Christmas party was a kettle drum. The bands that play as the soldiers and sailors march to church on Sundays have kettle drums, they also have bass drums, and something that looks like two pot covers. When the bandsman hits them together, they make a ringing sound. The soldiers march out of the Wellington Barracks and come along Gottingen Street. The Church of England soldiers turn down Russell Street and go to St. Mark's. The Catholic soldiers keep going along Gottingen Street to St. Joseph's. The band comes down as far as St. Mark's. Then two small groups leave at St. Mark's. One goes over to the Kaye Street Methodist Church, the other goes to Grove Presbyterian Church, which is further north. Then the sailors come up Russell Street with the band from the Cruiser *Niobe*. They also bring their mascot with them. It is a goat. The sailors split up and go to their churches. Billy Hayes told me that they tie the goat in his yard while they are in church.'

In 1917 the huge natural harbour of Halifax was the gateway to the expanding Dominion of Canada. The city residents occupied the land between Point Pleasant Park in the southend of the peninsula overlooking the entrance to the harbour and Negro Point in the northend overlooking the Bedford Basin. The business district was below the Citadel fortress.

Public buildings were built of stone and brick while the majority of homes were built of wood. In the southend, homes surrounded the hill of Fort Massey, while the homes in the Richmond District surrounded the hill of Fort Needham. That northend district was named after the piers where ships from Richmond, Virginia used to dock. [The city had yet to fill the peninsula and would not do so until the 1960s.] The surrounding communities including the Town of Dartmouth, on the opposite shore, sent their produce to the city market and their children to the city high school. Halifax provided many young people with their first employment away from small farming and fishing communities.

Some Richmond District Churches pre 1917.

Left:
Saint Joseph's Roman Catholic Church.

Below: Grove Presbyterian Church.

Above: Kaye Street Methodist Church.

The school system of Halifax was divided by gentlemen's agreement into public and Catholic schools because of the large Irish population; financing came from taxes. The Anglican Church of Canada in 1917 was the Church of England; the Presbyterians, Methodists and Congregationalists had not yet formed the United Church of Canada. Automobiles were referred to as 'motors.' A motor was still a luxury; the common form of transportation around the province was the train and freight was moved by the carload. Coal was king and after three years of war, soot covered many houses where peeling paint marked a shortage of materials for domestic use and the absence of a loved one serving king and country overseas.

View of Cheapside with Customs House (right) and Post Office (left). The motor car is parked correctly, driving was on the left in Nova Scotia until the 1920s.

Many people have not heard of the 'Great Disaster' at Halifax Harbour. There was so much going on at the time. World War I destroyed countries, royal dynasties, and sent millions of people on a journey that would eventually bring them to North America.

**A look back at 1917:**

January 1—Lieutenant Governor of Nova Scotia, the Honourable F. MacCallum Grant, appointed November 1916, hosts his first Levee at Government House.

January—Lt. Murray, son of Premier George Murray of Nova Scotia is wounded. [The war would claim over 60,000 of Canada's service personnel.]

February—British Royal Family changes name to Windsor from Wettin to distance themselves from German connections.

March—Czar of Russia abdicates.

April 6—United States of America enters the War

April 9—Easter Monday four Canadian Divisions of 10,000 men take Vimy Ridge, France, a feat the troops of France and Britain had been unable to do.

May—In good weather people in Halifax take the Beltline tram for excursions around the city.

July 1—50th Anniversary of Dominion of Canada.

July 10—First in series of convoys leave Sydney, Nova Scotia. The British Naval Authority had decided the best way to guarantee safety of ships across the North Atlantic is to group them in convoys especially from Sydney and the ice free winter harbour at Halifax.

July 25—Canadian Finance Minister Sir Thomas White introduces new 'temporary' income tax to pay for the war effort.

September—Knitting allowed during lectures in Halifax high schools, to make goods for soldiers overseas.

September 5—First convoy leaves Halifax.

October—Teams take to the ice as National Hockey League [NHL]

October—North and Grand Trunk consolidated with Intercolonial Railway into Canadian Government Railway [CGR].

October—First regular winter ferry service between New Brunswick and Prince Edward Island begins.

October 12—The Member of Parliament for Halifax, Sir Robert

Borden from Nova Scotia forms government in Ottawa [Unionist].

November 29—Members of Museum of Fine Arts gather in Halifax for annual meeting and opening of an art exhibit from Ottawa.

On December 1, 1917, visitors to Halifax see a bustling town with many homes preparing packages for overseas and waiting for return mail. The chill in the air heralded the excitement for the season fast approaching. Ships were arriving to join convoys.

December 1—The ship *Mont Blanc* leaves New York Harbour. On board had been loaded, without incident in American ports, 21,830 kegs and barrels of wet and dry picric acid, 682 cases of gun cotton, 5000 kegs and cases of TNT, and 494 drums of highly explosive benzol most of which are stacked on the open deck of the ship.

December 3—The ship *Imo* drops anchor in the Bedford Basin of Halifax harbour on way to pick up relief supplies in New York.

December 3—Naval authorities in Halifax are aware the *Mont Blanc* would arrive with cargo of explosives, no special plans are made as many munitions ships have made trips into Halifax Harbour and Bedford Basin during war.

December 5—*Imo* departure delayed, waiting for coal supply, must stay overnight in Bedford Basin.

December 5—*Mont Blanc* anchors outside main Halifax Harbour overnight due to closing of submarine nets.

December 5—Saint Mark's Church of England, Richmond District has evening fair.

December 5—Grove Presbyterian Church, Richmond District has celebration to mark paying off debt on buildings.

December 5—People cross town for evening theatre events.

December 6—Submarine nets open, shipping starts to move.

Sir Robert Borden, Premier of Canada.

A panorama of downtown Halifax looking west to the Citadel on a cold winter day c1913.

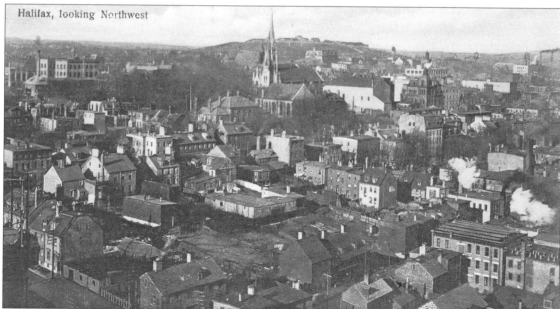

Halifax, looking Northwest

| Nova Scotia's Win-the-War Newspaper | THE HALIFAX HERALD | Nova Scotia's Win-the-War Newspaper |
|---|---|---|
| | ALL THE NEWS. HONEST VIEWS. HONEST ADVERTISING | |

FOUNDED FEBRUARY 14, 1875.     HALIFAX, CANADA, FRIDAY, DECEMBER 7, 1917     VOLUME XLIII, NO. 290.

# HALIFAX WRECKED

## More Than One Thousand Killed In This City, Many Thousands Are Injured And Homeless.

MORE than one thousand dead and probably five thousand injured, many of them fatally, is the result of the explosion yesterday on French steamship Mont Blanc, loaded with nitroglycerine and trinitrotuol. All of Halifax north and west of the depot is a mass of ruins and many thousands of people are homeless. The Belgian Relief steamer Imo, coming down from Bedford Basin, collided with the Mont Blanc. which immediately took fire and was headed in for Pier No. 8 and exploded. Buildings over a great area collapsed, burying men, women and children. Tug boats and smaller vessels were engulfed and then a great wave washed up over Campbell Road. Fires broke out and became uncontrollable, stopping the work of rescue. Not a house in Halifax escaped some damage, and the region bounded on the east by the harbor, south by North street and west by Windsor street, is absolutely devastated.

THE wounded and homeless are in different institutions and homes over the city. The Halifax Herald is collecting information regarding the missing, and citizens who have victims of the disaster at their homes are requested to telephone to The Herald office. Hundreds of the bodies which were taken from the ruins are unrecognizable and morgues have been opened in different parts of the city. Citizens' committees are being formed for rescue work. Bulletins will be issued thruout the day giving information for the assistance of those who have lost relatives and friends. While practically every home in the city is damaged, those who are able to give any temporary accommodation are asked to notify some of the committees.

Military and naval patrols are keeping order and superintending the rescue work.

Front page of the *Halifax Herald*, December 7, 1917.

Chapter 2

# DECEMBER 6 AND THE RICHMOND DISTRICT

*'Richmond with land to spare knew no overcrowding and was spared the greater city's problems. She could not boast of wealth nor complain of poverty. Here dwelt the artisan, the railroad man, the independent man of moderate means, the home maker, the man of enterprise building the city's newer part.'*

Reverend C.S. Crowdis, Minister, Grove Presbyterian Church, Richmond District, Halifax.

**Sugar Refinery, Richmond District.**

As Thursday, December 6, 1917 dawned, it was a clear day with no fog on the harbour and no snow on the ground. Some remember it as almost an Indian summer day, warm and sunny. With wood and coal burning stoves heating their homes, people prepared for work, school, daily activities. The *Mont Blanc*, munitions ship, moved into the harbour, the *Imo*, relief ship, prepared to leave.

The waterfront was busy with activity as shift changes were made. Morning prayers through the city were said for those overseas in the fields of war. Children greeted friends after finishing morning chores of filling wood bins and coal buckets. People reporting for work downtown would comment 'beautiful day.'

As the *Imo* entered the corner of the narrows it had to move slightly off course to make way for an American tramp steamship coming from along the piers to the right. The *Imo* then had to move further to the left to avoid a tugboat pulling two barges [equal in length to a 400-foot ship]. These movements put the *Imo* on the wrong side of the narrow channel. Unseen by the Captain and Pilot on the *Imo*, coming from the other direction, out of the sun, was the *Mont Blanc*.

The *Imo* had no cargo onboard, was riding high in the water and was difficult to steer. The *Imo* Captain was trying to get back to his side of the channel. The *Mont Blanc* Captain gave warning to the *Imo* to move out of the way. The sounds of ship whistles drew the attention of people onshore who realized the ships would collide. The *Imo* Captain reversed engines. The *Mont Blanc* Captain decided if the ship approaching was taking his side he would move across to the other side. Turning his ship he exposed the side of the *Mont Blanc* to the bow of the *Imo*. The two ships collided with the *Imo* digging through the steel plates of the *Mont Blanc*. As the reversed engines dragged the *Imo* away, the *Mont Blanc*'s cargo caught fire. The Captain and men of the *Imo* stayed on board their ship as there was no danger of sinking and they watched the scene unfold.

Soon the fire on the *Mont Blanc* was out of control. The Captain of the *Mont Blanc* ordered his men to abandon ship. They rowed hard to the sparsely populated shore of Dartmouth as the ship drifted toward the Richmond Piers and the industrial and residential Northend of Halifax.

With fire raging on the *Mont Blanc* small explosions occurred which sent barrels of benzol into the air like fireworks. This brought workers to warehouse doorways and residents to their windows. As Richmond District schools had not yet started for the day children raced down the streets telling their friends of the great excitement, of a ship on fire.

A call was made to the fire station and soon the clanging bells of the fire wagons attracted more people of the District to the scene. Yet in the other parts of Halifax very few people were aware of the ship on fire. The tugboat, *Stella Maris*, that had passed the *Imo* in the narrows anchored its barges and turned back to give assistance. Men of the British Royal Navy ship HMS *Highflyer* and the Royal Canadian Navy ship HMCS *Niobe* made their way to the burning *Mont Blanc* to tie lines onboard to pull the ship away from the wooden piers. Still the crowds grew larger, along north Barrington Street, at Mulgrave Park [a public square on the slope of the hill], in the windows and on roof tops of the industrial buildings. Very few were aware of the danger, no flag on the ship warned of munitions. The crew of the *Mont Blanc* reached the other shore, one man grabbed a child and ran to the trees followed by an anxious mother. The crew would give no other warning, panic had set in, they knew their cargo.

The fire debris of the *Mont Blanc* was now landing on the wooden piers; men were trying to do their duty; hundreds gathered to see the excitement. On the slopes of Fort Needham women and children looking through the windows of their homes saw the smoke rising high in the sky and stood hypnotized by the sight. Still, other parts of the city were unaware of a ship on fire.

A wireless operator, Vincent Coleman, overlooking the scene realized that morning trains would soon be moving along the rails by the burning ship. He sent a message 'Munitions ship on fire making for pier 8 Goodbye.'

At a few minutes after 9:00 a.m. on December 6, 1917, the munitions ship *Mont Blanc* exploded shattering into hot fragments of steel that rained down on the city like gunfire.

**The explosion caused three major forces to be released:**
A tidal wave in the area of the explosion ripped ships from their moorings and swept men, women and children off the lower streets and piers and drowned them in the harbour.

The ground shook like an earthquake and the tremor was felt as far away as the Cape Breton Islands, Prince Edward Island and New Brunswick cracking windows and rattling china.

The wind force of the explosion caused the most damage. At the centre of the blast the ten storey brick and stone sugar refinery completely collapsed, the Richmond piers splintered into ruins. As the wind blast hit the slope, wooden houses fell to the ground. Fort Needham hill blocked some of the force of the explosion and deflected it up into the sky. However, as the air pushed around and behind the hill, churches, schools and houses were smashed open. Throughout the rest of the city, windows shattered into a million fine pieces, doors blew into houses and chimneys fell to the ground.

In the Northend where the damage was greatest, the explosion killed many people instantly. Others were trapped in their ruined homes and soon the fires from the overturned wood and coal burning

Views of destroyed Gottingen Street house and store.

stoves and furnaces set the buildings ablaze. Men, women and children burned to death. Winter fuel supplies in the cellars would burn for days removing all trace of the occupants.

With word that ammunition magazines or other ships might explode, people were rushed away from the buildings and into open areas of parks, fields and commons. The injured moved south seeking help at doctors' houses and the hospitals. The morning and afternoon remained sunny. Help in town was quickly organized. With communications limited due to wires knocked down, the trains that were soon taking people to Truro for medical attention relayed the requests for help. That afternoon relief crews and supplies were sent from small towns and villages of Nova Scotia. By nightfall a severe snow storm added to the misery of those homeless, delayed outside help for the injured, and buried those trapped in the ruins of buildings.

That same evening, after sending messages offering help, the first of many relief trains from the United States of America would leave Boston.

On December 7, the scene in the Richmond District was one of desolation.

The following photos illustrate the statement of George Yates private secretary to Sir Robert Borden, who wrote of the disaster as 'too dreadful to admit of description in coherent, matter of fact English.'

### The fear of a second explosion on December 6th:

Fires surrounding the Ammunition Magazine at Wellington Barracks on Gottingen Street caused an evacuation which resulted in further suffering.

In *Halifax Herald* Dec. 11, 1917 'Extricated by Daughter from Wreckage'

'Mrs. Hayclock Wambolt 6 Bilby Street was buried under wreckage and had to be extricated by her daughter Nina. Mrs. Wambolt had her collarbone broken and when ordered to leave the city, walked to Rockingham... and from whence was driven in a lumber wagon to Hammond Plains... suffered intense pain for a day and a night before a doctor could be obtained.'

The Magazine was saved from fire by men of the 72nd Battalion of Ottawa.

Above: Searchers pose by a ruined house as a pig forages for food nearby.

Left: A photo from Colonel Low album, Reconstruction Office. The caption read: 'The only living members of a family return home and find insurance policy safe in drawer of broken dresser. In background ruins and narrows of harbour.' Many insurance companies in Canada and the U.S. would quickly advertise 'protect yourself from the next explosion.'

Scenes of destruction along rail, water and road.

Saint Joseph's School facing Kaye Street; most of the girls attending survived. The boys were to attend the afternoon shift, many of them died in the streets of Richmond watching the fire on the *Mont Blanc*. In the background is a view of St. Joseph's Church.

The ruins of St. Joseph's Roman Catholic Church.

### Richmond District Churches:

At Saint Joseph's Church mass had just ended. Father Gray was saved as he was standing under an archway. Mr. Ledieux of Cassavant Brothers, Ste. Hyacinthe, Quebec was in the loft making adjustments on the newly acquired organ when it overturned giving him slight injuries.

Saint Mark's Church of England burnt to the ground.

The Grove Presbyterian Church and manse were destroyed and the wife of Rev. C. S. Crowdis lost an eye.

Kaye Street Methodist Church, was destroyed. In the manse Rev. Swetnam saw his wife and son die under the piano they had just been playing, his daughter Dorothy was badly injured. All that was found intact in the wreckage was a cup inscribed 'Remember Me.'

People observing the scenes of the disaster would remark that the homes must have been poorly built to be destroyed so easily. They did not realize until later the strength of the explosion. Some people actually survived due to the fact the well-constructed homes on the hill withstood the blast allowing them to escape before the fires consumed the neighbourhood.

The last survivor would be dug out six days after the explosion. The last of the dead would be found almost a year later. Many people never sought help for their injuries and years later slivers of glass would emerge from their skin. Others would die of their injuries months into 1918. Some never recovered from the shock of their losses.

In 1918 the war ended and returning service personnel came home to rebuild their lives. They too suffered from horrible injuries. Throughout North America influenza broke out killing thousands, including those in Halifax who had never completely recovered from their explosion injuries. This ended any attempt to put a final toll on the victims of the disaster.

Over time a consensus was arrived at regarding the dead, injured and homeless. Of a population estimated at 60,000 in wartime 1917, there were approximately 2,000 dead, 9,000 injured and 25,000 left homeless.

The disaster now known as the 1917 Halifax Explosion is a story of great sadness. It is also the story of neighbourly help. It is a story of rebuilding and of continued thanks.

Above and left: The explosion sent the ship *Imo* onto the Dartmouth shore. The Captain and some of the crew of the *Imo* were killed. Only one of the crew of the *Mont Blanc* died as the Captain and crew had abandoned ship and fled to the woods. The munitions ship *Mont Blanc* shattered into pieces, her cannon flying 1-1/2 miles to the shore of Albro Lake, the anchor shank going 2-3/4 miles in the other direction landing on the west side of the Northwest Arm section of the harbour.

The first help after the explosion, of course, came from people in the Halifax area. The leaders of society took charge but it was only successful because everyone pulled together. Businessmen took up shovels to look for their workers' families. The poor made sacrifices to assist those who had been well-to-do. Society women stood shoulder to shoulder with their ladies' maids cleaning the wounded and caring for the orphaned. After years of sending loved ones away to war, the war had come home to their doorsteps and the people of Halifax and Dartmouth were ready to respond.

The disaster was of such magnitude that rebuilding without outside help would have been impossible. The people of Nova Scotia would do their part. As expected, Sir Robert Borden, Member of Parliament for Halifax for many years, offered the help of the entire Dominion of Canada. Individual provinces sent their donations quickly. Great Britain, the Mother Country and every part of the British Empire from the Colony of Newfoundland to far away Dominions of New Zealand and Australia sent funds for the relief of the people in Halifax.

Unexpected was the help that arrived from the United States of America, in particular, the New England States led by the example of the Governor of Massachusetts. The unsolicited help from Massachusetts was immediate and was done with charity in the best sense of the word. Respect for the dignity of the people receiving the funds was considered as the relief was sent, the reward was in the giving and not the thanks. This heartfelt gesture has left a lasting legacy in the history of Nova Scotia.

King Edward Hotel, Barrington Street at North Street, opposite the railway station.

The ruins of Grove Presbyterian Church where on the evening of Dec. 5, 1917 a celebration was held for paying off the building debt.

# BOSTON RUSHES RELIEF SPECIAL

## Trainload of Physicians, Nurses, Red Cross Workers and State Guard Officers on Way to Halifax

**BY ROY ATKINSON**

ON BOARD RELIEF TRAIN EN ROUTE TO HALIFAX, Dec. 6.— With the hope of breaking all speed records between Boston and Halifax

It was said tonight that another train will follow with supplies tomorrow.

During the time that the relief party is in Halifax the cars will be used as headquarters for workers and members of the press.

The train is made up of two baggage

Headings from *Boston Post*, December 7, 1917.

Chapter 3

# MASSACHUSETTS TO THE RESCUE

*'organize a relief train and send word to Wolfville and Windsor to round up all doctors, nurses, and Red Cross supplies possible to obtain. No time to explain details but list of casualties is enormous.'*

George Graham, General Mgr. of Dominion Atlantic Railway, walked and ran 3 miles, from Halifax to Rockingham Station to send his message.

Child patient photographed by Nathaniel Morse, one of the doctors of the Massachusetts State Guard.

The wireless message was picked up by operators along the eastern seaboard and passed on to various authorities. Boston received the news 2 hours after the explosion. At the State House, His Excellency, Governor Samuel W. McCall was informed and he soon organized relief efforts. He sent the following telegram to the Mayor of Halifax:

'Understand your city in danger from explosion and conflagration. Reports only fragmentary. Massachusetts ready to go the limit in rendering every assistance you may be in need of. Wire me immediately.'

Not receiving a reply as the wires were down in Halifax, the Governor sent through the government at Washington this message by wireless:

'Since sending my telegram this morning offering unlimited assistance, an important meeting of citizens has been held and Massachusetts stands ready to offer aid in any way you can avail yourself of it. We are prepared to send forward immediately a special train

with surgeons, nurses and other medical assistance, but await advices from you.'

Still not receiving a reply the Governor sent this third message:

'Realizing that time is of the utmost importance we have not waited for your answer but have dispatched the train.

Samuel W. McCall, Governor, Commonwealth of Massachusetts.'

At first Halifax citizens were dazed and quiet after the explosion. Soon survival instincts took over. As a military town and capital city there were organizations already in place to give assistance. There were also men on ships in the harbour waiting to depart for the war who were able to come to the aid of the city. Within fifteen minutes of the explosion the ship, USS *Old Colony*, in harbour awaiting repairs before leaving for England, sent two landing parties ashore with doctors and emergency kits. Later the ship would receive 150 of the injured.

## MAP SHOWING SECTION OF HALIFAX DEVASTATED BY EXPLOSION AND FIRE, INDICATED BY SHADED PORTION

*The Boston Globe*, December 8, 1917 map of Halifax.

Gottingen at the corner of Kenny Street showing the collapsed manse of Grove Presbyterian.

The US Coast Guard Cutter *Morrill* also sent a landing party to shore and in the harbour assisted the American steamship *Saranac* that was drifting for rocks.

Throughout the day soldiers and sailors worked in the ruins of the Richmond District. A description of what happened next is in the official history of the disaster written by Professor Archibald MacMechan of Dalhousie University:

'It was a long hard day. Every hour and every minute had its own particular difficulty or problem. By nine o'clock at night staff and H.Q. men were pretty well exhausted. All the available troops had been working very hard, and, if they were to continue next day, they must have sleep and rest. The usual guards at various points had to be maintained, just as if nothing had happened. The total number of troops available had been diminished by a long list of killed or wounded. The whole city was "wide

# HORRORS OF HALIFAX UNEQUALED IN WAR

## Harrowing Scenes Surpass Any On Battlefields, Says Survivor

## Frenzied Men Rush About Wildly in Search Of Lost Loved Ones

A photograph titled 'Bodies taken from ruin of the fire area' that was featured in the book, *Heart Throbs of the Halifax Horror* published in 1918.

Left: *The Boston Globe*, December 8, 1917.

open," and night had come on. Colonel Thompson and his staff were "combing their brains" how to get the necessary guards, when there was a knock at the door of the office, and in came two American naval officers, Captain Stanford E. Moses, of the USS *Von Steuben* and Captain Howard Symington of the USS *Tacoma*. They asked, "Is there anything we can do?" The answer was, "Can you give me any men to patrol the streets?" "Any number?" "Can you give me two hundred and fifty?" The answer was, "Yes," and almost before the Headquarters staff could realize it, the efficient Americans had the required force of blue-jackets and marines on shore and had taken over the guardianship of the Halifax streets, thus affording the wearied Canadians the rest and sleep they needed so badly for the toil of the terrible next day, the day of the blizzard. This thoughtful consideration on the part of the American officers is characteristic of the people they represented, and was manifested in a thousand ways by the measures of relief which they put in operation later.'

[The USS Cruiser *Tacoma* had felt the concussion wave 52 miles off Halifax. The *Von Steuben* suffered minor damage when the steamer *Northwind* drifted into it.]

As the Americans assisted, meetings were held in Halifax. The Mayor was away, so the Chair was taken by Nova Scotia's Lieutenant Governor F. MacCallum Grant. Unknown to these meetings was the action being taken in Boston by the Governor of Massachusetts and the fact that a train was on the way.

On board the first American Medical Relief train were:

'Mr. A.C. Ratchesky [the Governor's representative]
Surgeons and Doctors (All of the Massachusetts State Guard).
Major Harold G. Giddings (in command), Major Edward A. Supple,
Major Donald V. Baker (Surgeon in Chief), Major George W. Morse.
Major Peter Owen Shea, Captain Edward F. Murphy (Adjutant).
Captain Thomas F. Harrington (Physician in Chief)
Captain John W. Dewis.

Captain Robert G. Loring (Ophthalmologist)
Captain DeWitt G. Wilcox.
Captain Nathaniel N. Morse (Anesthetist).
Quartermasters Department: Captain Benjamin D. Hyde and
Captain Henry G. Lapham.
Red Cross Representatives: John F. Moors, Chairman, C.C. Carsten,
Secretary, Miss Katherine McMahon, Associate Director, Civilian
Relief Committee (Metropolitan District). J. Prentice Murphy,
Secretary, Children's Aid Society. Wm. H. Pear of the Boston
Provident Association.
Miss Marion Rowe of the Boston Associated Charities.
Nurses: Miss Elizabeth Peden (in charge). Miss Nellie P. Black,
Miss Edith F. Perkins, Miss Charlotte Naismith, Miss Elizabeth
Choate, Miss Marion Nevens, Miss Jessie McInness, Miss Mary A.
Davidson, Miss Florence B. McInness, Miss Caroline E. Carlton.
Railroad Officials: G.V. Worthen, Boston & Maine Railroad,
M.L. Harris, Maine Central Railroad (left train at Portland).
E.F. Sturdee, Canadian Pacific, Boston,
C.K. Howard, Canadian Government Railways, Boston.
Representatives of the Press: A.J. Philpott, *Boston Globe*, Richard
W. Sears, *Boston American*., R.W. Simpson, Associated Press, J.V.
Keating, *Boston Herald*., Roy Atkinson, *Boston Post*.'

Having received permission to pass all other traffic the train sped
through the snow to reach Halifax on December 8. Those on board the
Boston train quickly saw the situation was much worse than imagined.
The Americans immediately set about fitting in where they could help.
The newsmen sent stories back to alert the citizens of the United States
of the great need of the 'suffering people of Halifax.'

In the report of Mr. Ratchesky to the Governor of Massachusetts:
    'We arrived at the terminus about 7 o'clock. Mr. Howard and I left

A postcard showing the wrecked North Street Train Station.
Relief trains were diverted to the new southend rail yard.

the train, and as well as we could, proceeded up the main road to the
building which had been taken by the Canadian Government Railways
for temporary headquarters. It was our good fortune to find there
C.A. Hayes, General Manager of the Canadian Government Railways,
the first man we met in Halifax and to whom I showed your letter to
the Mayor. He was so affected that tears streamed down his cheeks. He
arose and greeted me with: "Just like the people of good old
Massachusetts. ..." He gave us the use of his temporary wires, which
had been connected with City Hall, and informed us that the private
[rail] car of Sir Robert L. Borden, Premier of Canada, was on the
tracks very near to ours.

    ...Mr. Hayes dispatched a message to the Premier, with the sug-
gestion that members of the relief party from Massachusetts would be
very glad to call upon him in his car as soon as possible. His answer
came most informally. He joined us in person in a very few minutes,
expressing to us in appropriate words his profound appreciation of the
quick action on the part of the Commonwealth of Massachusetts...

He asked us to join him proceeding to City Hall in order to present your letter to the Mayor and learn what disposition we should make of our party and supplies.'

Later in the report of Mr. Ratchesky:

'Major Giddings and Colonel McKelvey Bell, acting at my request, in company with leading doctors of the city, found a large building near the center of the city known as the Bellevue Building and used as the Officers Club house. The building was turned over to us in very bad condition, not a door or window remaining whole, and water and ice on the floor of every room. Apparently, under ordinary circumstances, it would have been impossible to have put into shape for a long time. But by 12:30 o'clock, on the first day of our arrival, Major Giddings with his quartermasters, ably assisted by about fifty of the crew of the United States training ship *Old Colony*,... together with a company of Canadian soldiers... immediately set to work cleaning the rooms, covering the windows with paper and boards, as best they could, washing floors and woodwork, and removing all furniture to the upper part of the building. British Military Stores Depot furnished full equipment in the way of bedside tables, rubber sheets, dishes and tableware. The British Authorities also furnished to the hospital unit cooks and kitchen utensils, besides supplying the hospital with food from its commissary and detailing a corps of trained clerks and orderlies.'

Major Giddings, Commander of the Massachusetts Medical Unit in his report stated:

'We took formal possession of the Bellevue Military Hospital on the morning of December 9. That afternoon the hospital was officially visited by Sir Robert Borden, Premier of Canada. After his inspection His Excellency issued the following statement: "This afternoon I visited the hospital established at Bellevue by the Massachusetts hospital unit. They took possession yesterday...and within a few hours had every

arrangement made for receiving patients, of whom nearly seventy-five are now being accommodated. ...The hospital is a triumph of organizing ability!"...'

## Some help by land, two ships by sea:

As the Massachusetts relief train was heading to Halifax a meeting was organized in Boston.

At Faneuil Hall in Boston a mass meeting was called 'in the interests of Halifax sufferers,' a relief fund was set up and $100,000 was raised the first day.

The results of the meeting included sending supply ships to Halifax.

The *Calvin Austin*: 'Mr. Endicott had obtained a relief ship, the *Calvin Austin*, and Saturday morning papers in Boston carried notices that supplies would be collected for her. Before the day was over, the depot had overflowed. Mounted police had to control the crowd. A society lady took off her fur coat and gave it to the cause. One reporter describing the scene wrote: "A steady line of automobiles, trucks, taxicabs and other vessels streamed to the wharf, almost to the moment of sailing, and deposited their loads, while hundreds came afoot or by trolley with their contributions. As the steamer started on her trip, with a big Red Cross flag streaming out from her masthead, a lusty cheer went up from the crowd of workers and spectators who lined the docks." Three days later, after a rough passage, she was cheered again when she arrived in Halifax Harbour.'

Above: A photo from the *Boston Globe*, December 8, 1917. The caption read: 'In the hours last night while the Red Cross train was being stocked Mrs. Samuel McCall, [wife of the Governor] at left, and Mrs. George Mixter passed out coffee and sandwiches to workers on station platform.'

**RELIEF FOR HALIFAX**

The Management of the
**COPLEY THEATRE**
Announce a Special Performance of
**"The Man Who Stayed at Home"**
by the
**HENRY JEWETT PLAYERS**
(Who have volunteered their services)
**Sunday Evening, December 9th**
The entire proceeds to be given to the Halifax Sufferers
**ORDER SEATS NOW**
Box Office Open Sunday at 12 Noon
Tel. 3518 Back Bay

The following story appeared in the *Boston Evening Globe*, Wednesday, December 12, 1917:

'BOSTON RELIEF SHIP ARRIVES AT HALIFAX

HALIFAX, NS., DEC 12—The Boston relief ship *Calvin Austin* entered the harbour today.

The arrival of the *Calvin Austin* was made the occasion of a demonstration at the pier.

The vessel, bringing clothing, food, and more important still, glass and the materials greatly needed, was welcomed by huge crowds who cheered the ship, the captain, the crew and her precious cargo.

The relief work is being developed along better organized lines daily. Committees of Halifax men are in immediate direction of the work, those from New England serving in an advisory capacity with the exception, of course, of the physicians and nurses who are still occupied to the limit of physical endurance....'

The *Northland* [from State House files]:
'Mr. H. Endicott asked H.J. McAlman, President of the Massachusetts Automobile Dealers Association to buy $25,000 worth of trucks and see that they were loaded aboard the Northland. A few hours later McAlman walked into Endicott's state house office and told him: "We bought the trucks, we hired 10 first-class chauffeurs to go with them…and if you'll break down certain stiff laws we'll send gasoline enough along in them, or being carried on them to run "em for awhile."

The state sent as "an absolute gift," five Republics, three Whites and two Stewarts, with 10 drums of gasoline. The trucks carried signs reading "Massachusetts to Halifax."

On December 13, the *Northland* dropped anchor in Halifax harbour next to the *Calvin Austin*.'

Left: A advertisement in the *Boston Globe*, December 8, 1917.

## A selection of telegrams offering American aid:

Washington D.C.
Dec. 7th 1917

To Lieut. Governor, Halifax N.S.
American Red Cross sending three trainloads clothing, bedding and hospital supplies, about one hundred doctors and nurses and twenty experienced disaster relief workers.... all these resources at service yourself and your stricken city.

W. Frank Persons,
Director General Civilian Relief, American Red Cross

Boston Mass:
Dec. 10th 1917

Am shipping tonight by freight four animal drawn ambulances; drivers and animals to be provided in Halifax; also X-Ray apparatus with personnel due to arrive Halifax Wednesday morning. Shipment consigned to you.

New York.
Dec. 10th 1917

To Mayor, Halifax N.S.
We offer five hundred dollars in drugs and medicines, wire us your needs.

McKesson & Robbins,
Wholesale Druggists.'

Reply:
Church of England Institute,
Halifax, N.S.,
Dec. 10th 1917

To McKesson & Robbins. Wholesale Druggists. New York
Many thanks for kind offer. Please send ether, chloroform, tincture of iodine and antistreptococcic serum.

McKelvey Bell, Lieut.-Co.,
Chairman Medical Relief Committee

View of ruins looking south east from Agricola Street to Almon Street. The buildings in this photograph were repaired.

A truck donated by Massachusetts viewed in front of the Queen Hotel, Hollis Street. The sign on the side of truck read 'Massachusetts to Halifax.'

Soon other trains of relief workers would arrive from across Canada and the United States and it was time for the first group to return home.

From Major Giddings' Report:

'On the morning of December 12, after a conference with Mr. Ratchesky, it seemed that the situation as regards to medical aid was so well in hand that our unit might with propriety withdraw....

The work of no individual member of the unit stands out pre-eminently. Perhaps the one surgeon whose services were of the most help was Captain Loring. This was because of the great number of eye injuries... Captain Loring was called upon to do work not only at Bellevue but at the Military Hospital, the Halifax Infirmary and at Camp Hill Hospital, where he saw, at the request of Lieutenant-Governor Calvin Coolidge of Massachusetts, Miss Bertha Ferguson, an American girl of Boston....'

From Major Giddings report regarding Dec. 13:

'That evening His Honor Lieutenant-Governor and Mrs. F. MacCallum Grant, of the Province of Nova Scotia, gave to our party a delightful and informal dinner, which was in the nature of an official recognition of the work the unit had done. Lacking other means of conveyance to the Governor's home, the doctors were carried in one of the new automobile trucks, the gift of our State, which that day had reached Halifax from Boston.

...The occasion, at which cordiality was the keynote, was a most delightful one...A toast was proposed by His Honor the Governor to "The President and the King," and both the British and the American national anthems were sung. Thus, the event assumed certain international significance. In fact, Governor Grant during the course of his remarks expressed what we all felt, namely, that, lamentable as the disaster was, it had undoubtedly furthered the cordial relations between Canada and the United States.'

Government House, Halifax, as it appeared in the *New York Times*. Many newspapers used pre explosion photographs from souvenir booklets to illustrate their reports. No photo was taken to show its 900 broken panes of glass.

A formal resolution was made by the Relief Committee:

'Halifax, N.S. December 13, 1917

H. G. Giddings, Major, Medical Corps, State of Massachusetts, Halifax, N. S.

Dear Major Giddings:- At a meeting of the Executive of the Relief Committee, held this afternoon, it was the earnest desire of the members that before the Medical Corps of the State of Massachusetts took its departure from Halifax a formal minute should be placed on our records, which in the future will be the basis of the official history of the Halifax disaster, expressing the committee's deep appreciation of the prompt and humane action of the authorities in Boston in dispatching your corps to Halifax, and of the professional efficiency and noble spirit which you and all members of your unit have exhibited since coming to our stricken city. We shall always bare you in grateful remembrance, and wish you a safe journey home.

Yours truly,

R. T. MacIlreith,

Chairman, Relief Committee'

Major H.G. Giddings sent telegrams following his Unit's return to Massachusetts:

'To Chairman Medical Relief Committee.

Dec. 16th 1917

Colonel F. McKelvey Bell

Halifax N.S.

At Hospital you will find package of cigarettes, chocolates etc. for me from Colonel Brooks who wishes you to accept it with his compliments for personal or any other use you see fit. We arrived home safely and all so glad of opportunity to contribute our bit.

H. G. Giddings.'

The reply:

'Dec. 17th 1917
Major H.G. Giddings,
Adjutant, Boston Mass.

Very many thanks for your kind telegram. Articles mentioned will be turned over to doctors and nurses at hospital. Kindest regards.

McKelvey Bell, Lieut.-Col.
Halifax Medical Relief Committee'

On December 17 more help is offered:

'Friend wishes to contribute toys for one hundred blind children. To whom shall we send them?

H. G. Giddings,
Brighton, Mass. U.S.A.'

The reply:

'Please send toys Rehabilitation Committee, Army and Navy Club, Halifax. Thank your friend from the Committee. May his name be given.

McKelvey Bell Lieut.-Col.,
Chairman Medical Relief Committee'

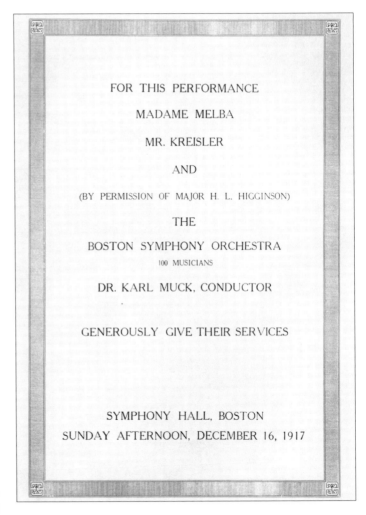

FOR THIS PERFORMANCE

MADAME MELBA

MR. KREISLER

AND

(BY PERMISSION OF MAJOR H. L. HIGGINSON)

THE

BOSTON SYMPHONY ORCHESTRA

100 MUSICIANS

DR. KARL MUCK, CONDUCTOR

GENEROUSLY GIVE THEIR SERVICES

SYMPHONY HALL, BOSTON
SUNDAY AFTERNOON, DECEMBER 16, 1917

A popular way to raise funds for relief was to stage an entertainment. The above page is from a programme printed for a 'concert given for the Relief of Sufferers from the Recent Disaster in Halifax Nova Scotia' just 10 days after explosion. Nellie Melba of Melba Toast and Peach Melba fame was the most famous of the performers to donate their talents.

## A notice from Salem, Massachusetts:

'HALIFAX NEEDS YOUR HELP
Give and Give At Once

The Salem Red Cross branch and Public Safety Committee urges all citizens of Salem and vicinity to do its share at this time in relieving the terrible distress resulting from the catastrophe at Halifax. No words are necessary to describe the crying need of all kinds of assistance.

You can render immediate aid by contributing warm clothing or other supplies to the local committee....'

It was a happy coincidence for the author to do a tour in 1996 and meet Henry Handly, a spry gentleman who was 16 years old in Salem, Mass. in 1917. At 95, he clearly remembered that as a boy scout he had collected for the relief of Halifax. 79 years later he was visiting the city he had assisted.

## The Farrell's of 30 1/2 Albert Street:

'My mother always claimed the virtue of being the first one up Young Street with me in her arms. She walked straight out to North West Arm carrying me. While waiting with others to get out to Chocolate Lake, a large wagon came along and mother saw Aunt Babe in it and waved and called out to her. Aunt Babe didn't pay any attention and mother said to a gentleman who stood beside her, "My, people are strange, that is my sister-in-law and she didn't recognize me."

The man replied, "If you don't mind my saying so. 'You are as black as the ace of spades." She had fire-powder all over her....

In the meantime my Dad, Jim Farrell, [a painter by trade] was together with my Uncle John looking for Mother and Aunt Babe. Eventually they found them in an army tent on the Halifax Commons. Uncle John developed the flu or galloping consumption and died.

Mother's father went over to get her cousin who was in a carriage and a chimney fell down on them and broke their necks. They lived on Needham Street. Aunt Josie was deafened.

Mother always spoke with reverence of the U.S.A. people because they sent Stucco Homes and furniture all free. Those homes are still in the Hydrostone Places but they were sold privately. We were never allowed in the parlour until we were 10 or so because it had Massachusetts furniture in it.'

Remembered by Sister Teresa Clare Farrell, Sister of Charity who was nine months old on Dec. 6, 1917.

Left: Furniture supply depot. The Massachusetts Relief Committee felt that providing a variety of furnishings would allow survivors to choose what they wanted.

The American response to Halifax was quick, sincere and generous. It can be summed up in the last 7 verses of the *Record of Halifax Explosion* written by Clark Hall:

'When good old Boston heard the news,
She answered like a flash,
And sent us food and clothing
Likewise men and cash.

As soon as they received the news,
Without the least delay,
They got their cars in readiness
And started on their way.

God bless our neighbours to the South,
God bless them one and all
Who responded so magnificently
To humanity's urgent call.

Where'er that spangled banner floats,
On water or on land,
You'll always find them ready
To reach out a helping hand.

They sent us their trained nurses
With a brotherly, Christian will,
And in the medical line, the best
Of Massachusetts' skill.

They attended to our cut and torn
In an earnest, faithful manner,
Those ministering angels in our midst,
From beneath that starry banner.

We never shall forget them
Till we go to our grave.
And may the flag of freedom
Forever o'er them wave.'

Chapter 4

# STORIES OF HALIGONIANS

*'If we at the southend had known that northenders were buried under their houses and being burned to death, no doubt we would have done more to help them.'*

Stanley MacKenzie, President, Dalhousie University

Remains of a house on Duffus Street in the Richmond District.

But on that day many did not know what was the most urgent to be done and just did the best they could. The explosion had common elements that many remember, the cloud rising above the city, the harbour waters covered in wreckage, furnishings and bodies. Glass shattered in piles like fine snow, crumbling plaster making it hard to see; telephone lines were down and gas cut off as the pipes were broken.

There was the oily soot that rained down on the city; the thought that the enemy had arrived and worse was to come; the tapping of hammers all day and night as people tried to close in broken windows and doors; the snow and the cold of the next days.

Along with the collective experience there are also the personal stories, different for each involved because of location and luck.

**Murphy's of 29 Russell Street:**

In the words of Walter Murphy Jr.: [The Catholic Boys School was being rebuilt after a fire—they were sharing St. Joseph's Girls School, in separate shifts of course!]

'It was the boys' turn to go to school in the afternoon. I didn't have to be up and out in time to get to school for twenty minutes to nine. The twenty minutes is for prayers and religious instruction.

I was upstairs in the front bedroom, my mother was downstairs in the kitchen, my father was a Commercial Traveller and was away. My sister, Mary, was two years old and her cot was in that room, when she stood up her head was even with the top of the cot's railing.

My mother's sister stayed with us. She was a milliner and she had her own business. Her work place was in the Green Lantern building on Barrington Street. People called her Anna, but her name was

Walter Murphy Jr. and his sister Mary on step with god-mother. Temporary quarters at great-uncle's house, Woodhill Street, winter 1917-18.

Rented quarters on Maynard Street, 1918-19. New clothes and shoes look a little large on Walter Jr., Mary looks just fine.

Return home to Russell Street, 1920. Mary with Walter Jr. New house was built where other had burnt on Dec. 6. In background is Mrs. Annie Oaks tiny tarpaper house which Mary Murphy remem-bered as warm and cozy. Many families did not rebuild in the Richmond District and lots remained vacant until World War II.

Walter Murphy Sr. with his 3 year old daughter, Mary, overlooking reconstruction in spring 1918. Mary is in her new outfit.

really Anastasia. Aunt Anna came into the room where my sister and I were. She was on her way to work, and was standing alongside my sister's cot saying good-bye when there was the biggest bang I ever heard in my life. The next thing I was on my hands and knees on the floor, and a piece of wood hit me on the back of the head and cut it. I looked up and there was a hole in the roof and I could see the sky. The chimney had been knocked over and broke some of the roof rafters and it was one of them that had struck me a glancing blow. I followed Aunt Anna over to the windows, the glass was all gone, and the street outside was filled with wreckage. The stairs were covered with broken plaster and after the first few steps there was so much plaster we could only slide the rest of the way. We got to the lower hall, the base burner (that's a stove that burns hard coals and keeps the house warm all night) was knocked on its side.

We got into the kitchen and there was my mother lying in a heap under the sink and a lot of boards from the wainscoting over her. I helped Aunt Anna with moving the boards off my mother and Aunt Anna got my mother up on her feet, but she didn't know what had happened or what was going on. She must have struck her head on the corner of the sink when she was knocked down, because she had a curved cut on the back of her head, and must have been suffering from concussion.

All Aunt Anna could do was hold her and try to get her out of the house. We went into the back porch, the roof and back wall were still there, but both ends had been blown completely away. There were men going up the street from the work places, one man stopped and helped Aunt Anna get Mom out of the house and down on the ground, and then went on his way. The next thing Mom did was to try to go into the house next door and Aunt Anna doing her best to stop that.

All this time I was looking north and could see the flames from the houses burning. Then my uncles (my mother's brothers) James and Richard Spence arrived. Uncle Jim took my sister and we all started up the hill, I remember seeing a piece of steel plate I would judge about three feet square lying in the middle of the street.

We went as far as Hubley's store, an automobile came by, my mother was put on it, and because of the cut on my head I was put on it also. We were taken to the Victoria General Hospital. Everyone was busy there, but there was no panic. A doctor stitched the cut in my mother's head, and they did mine. Late in the afternoon, my people came and got me and took me to my grand-uncle's home on Woodhill Street. It was nice and bright in the morning, but was getting overcast and cloudy.'

Mary Murphy was only two at the time of the great disaster so does not remember the adventure as her brother did. However, she did listen closely to the stories told over the years by others including her mother. Her mother was doing the morning dishes and was thinking of Christmas preparations. 'My mother next woke up in hospital. When someone told her that there had been an explosion, she thought they meant her house alone had blown up. Maybe the hot water tank. Mother slept through visit of an important lady [probably the Duchess of Devonshire] and woke to having a flower left on her hospital bed. On the morning of Dec. 6, my mother was not recognized by her brothers James and Richard coming up Russell Street because she and Anna were blackened by soot.'

Mary Murphy was uninjured and was taken by a family to the village of Prospect where, she was later told, she would accept no sweets unless passed to her on a plate. Days later she would be reunited with her family. Some days after the explosion Uncle Richard Spence would be found standing in the street unable to move as shock had finally taken effect, he would recover.

Mary and Walter's father, Walter Sr. was a Commercial Traveller of Propriety Medicine and was in Newfoundland that fateful day. He had difficulty receiving word of what had happened to his family and returned as quickly as possible. Mary and Walter's uncle Patrick Murphy, his wife Katie, and uncle Martin Murphy and his wife Mary were killed in the explosion. The bodies of cousins, Wilfred and Norbert, were never found.

Mary Murphy remembers Christmas as a time people would reminisce about those who died and what Christmas had been like before the disaster. Extra big presents were made for those in the family left orphaned.

Mary and Walter's family home burnt to the ground that day and their mother would often speak of all that was lost. Eventually the family would consist of four boys and Mary. While mothers leave many things to their daughters the only pre 1917 items of the Murphy's to survive were a glass sent with jelly to a sick friend at Wellington Barracks and a small silver pot that had been at a relative's store for polishing.

**More on the Murphy's:**

Mary Murphy's cousins' story: 'Agnes Murphy left for school on December 6, 1917. Her mother called for her to wait for her little sister Theresa. Those were the last words Agnes was to hear from her mother. Mrs. Murphy died in the fiery ruins of the family home at 35 Acadia Street. Agnes' father, a railway worker, died two weeks after the explosion from injuries caused by the explosion. Three of the four children were brought up at Saint Joseph's Orphanage. Agnes joined the Sisters of Mount Carmel, teaching and nursing in Louisiana, retiring in 1990.' Sister Agnes made many return trips to Halifax to visit cousins in Saint Joseph's Parish.

In the files of the Halifax Relief Commission two items directly mention the Murphy family: 1. The Acadia Street land of Kathleen Murphy, Spinster, Agnes, Theresa, and Cecil was sold to the Relief Commission for $2,200.00 in full settlement of claim by their guardian Uncle Walter T. Murphy. 2. a permit given for a house at 29 Russell Street to Walter T. Murphy with the stipulation that it have a hip roof.

And in the Mortuary record, those 'not found' were added. It included '#1328 Wilfred Murphy, age 11, 33 Duffus Street identified by W.T. Murphy. #1329 Norbert Murphy, age 10, 35 Acadia Street identified by W.T. Murphy.' Years later W. T. Murphy's daughter, Mary would have a conversation with a member of the Creighton family who mentioned that two bodies were found in their store that could not be identified. Mary remembered being told that is where her two playful cousins were last seen heading on Dec. 6.

As for all the survivors still living in Halifax, World War II would bring back memories of 1917. In July 1945 the munitions depot caught fire and rocked the city with explosions breaking many windows and sending people fleeing to the open. As Mr. Walter Murphy Sr., by then bedridden, was being carried on a mattress out to a truck by soldiers he called to his family, 'Don't leave the house, that's how we lost the other one.' In later years Mary Murphy and her brothers watched with pride as their mother unveiled a plaque to the disaster in the Memorial Chapel of the rebuilt Saint Joseph's Church.

In the 1940s Mary Murphy (right) and friends would go for Sunday walks to the Bayers Road monument that marks one of the burial sites of the unidentified dead of the disaster. Here in paupers' grounds are the coffins turned away at Fairview Lawn Cemetery that had already taken many burials which could not be paid for. This site could be the final resting place of the two cousins, Wilfred and Norbert.

## The Coleman's of 31 Russell Street:

Vincent Coleman, a wireless operator, was at work at the Canadian Government Railways office behind piers 8 and 9. With others he was aware of the fire on the *Mont Blanc*. His telegraphed message 'Munitions ship on fire making for Pier 8 Goodbye' saved the people on the St. John Express Train. He was killed by the explosion. A notice in the newspaper read, 'Coleman, Vincent funeral Sunday Dec. 9, 2:30 from home of H.E. O'Toole, brother-in-law, 126 Edward Street.'

Vincent Coleman wireless operator.

The story on Mr. Coleman in the *Evening Mail* Dec. 10 was titled 'A hero in death as in Life' and included: 'Mr. Coleman was man who in July last jumped on runaway engine and stopped it in time to save collision with suburban train.'

The article also reported:

'To Editor:

I would appreciate highly if the relief Committee will ascertain whether or not any of his family are left alive and if so to give them special attention. Supervisor CGR Truro....'

Mr. Coleman's wife was badly injured; their five children were only slightly injured.' [One son survived after serving mass, another altar boy Leo Fultz was not so fortunate.]

A notice later appeared in the 'Personals' Jan. 7, 1918:

'The many friends of Mrs. Vincent Coleman now with her mother Eleanor O'Toole 126 Edward Street will be gratified to learn that she and her children are rapidly recovering from the injuries received in the explosion. Mrs. Coleman speaks in terms of deep gratitude of the many kindnesses of friends.'

Mrs. Coleman would remarry; her second husband, Mr. Jackson also a survivor would die in 1923 due to falling between moving cars in a Halifax rail yard; this was blamed on an arm that was injurjed in the explosion. Mrs. Coleman Jackson lived to over ninety years of age.

## The John Gammon Family of 39 1/2 Union Street:

At nine o'clock, just minutes before the explosion, naval divers from HMCS *Niobe* were working on the concrete foundations of a crane bed off the Dockyard pier. Chief Master at Arms John Gammon, RCN of HMCS *Niobe* was in charge of the detail that consisted of two divers and six sailors to man the pumps and air lines. The pumps, manned by hand, stood in a wood and corrugated iron shelter.

The party had been so busy in their work that they were not aware of the ship on fire. One diver was underwater, the second diver was on the ladder when the explosion occurred and was thrown into the water. The two sailors helping the divers and those manning the pumps were killed. John Gammon and Able Seaman Walter Critch RCN were hit by the blast but survived.

Walter Critch went to the shed, moved some timbers and found the pump undamaged. He held up wreckage with one hand and with the other he turned the wheel on the pumps to keep a small amount of air going to the divers.

John Gammon quickly went down the ladder as the water level decreased during the tidal wave. He found the divers alive but tangled in their life lines and air hoses. Gammon was able to untangle them and assist them up to the pier as the harbour waters returned and

A model at the Maritime Command Museum showing how John Gammon and Walter Critch rescued divers at dockyard pier Dec. 6, 1917.

crashed over them. He unscrewed their face glasses and left Critch to take care of them. Seeing smoke rise from the Richmond District he went to his home on Union Street to see if his wife and two youngest children were safe. He found the flats completely demolished and no sign of life. He went to St. Joseph's School on Kaye Street to search for his two older daughters; they were not there.

The next day John Gammon received news that his 7 year old daughter, Dorothy, was with a family. Eva May, 5 years old was in the care of the Sisters at Mount Saint Vincent. Two days after the explosion Gammon located his badly injured wife in a hospital. Fredd, 3 years old and Laura, 14 months, were never found.

John Gammon and Walter Critch later received awards for their brave rescue work on the pier.

**From the Fraser Harris Report:**

'Army—Private Myra of the C.A.M.C. worked continuously at rescue work for forty eight hours without a rest before he reported. It was then found that he had his left eye exceedingly badly injured with glass, the drum of one ear ruptured, two large fragments of glass in his left knee. The injured eye had to be removed on January 24th. A case like this is easily recorded but it is not so easy to realize the high degree of quiet heroism which it represents. It is typical of the stoic devotion to duty which characterized not a few of the voluntary workers on that dreadful day.'

Guard at Wellington Gate, Gottingen Street. Many military men were injured or killed. Some could only be identified as sailors by their bell-bottom pants. The soldiers at Wellington Barracks stood at their gate on December 6th giving out blankets and bandages to the crowds passing from the Richmond District.

Tents of the 85th Battalion on the Halifax Commons in 1916. The next year the explosion would force some of their families to stay in similar tents through cold nights.

In the background left to right are houses on Cunard Street, the Armouries and the Park Presbyterian Church on North Park Street.

### Beed Family of 53 Gerrish Street:

Explosion experiences as told to the author by his grandmother Mary Ann 'Min' [Mulcahie] Beed, his aunt Mary Beed [Gordon] and his cousin Esther Beed [Lynch.]

When Bridget [Stokes] Beed's husband George died in 1901, she moved with her two sons John and George to a large house on Gerrish Street. When her sons married, their wives and eventually children would also live with her.

John A. joined the 85th Nova Scotia Highland Battalion. In 1916 his group tented on the Halifax Commons. The Battalion then moved on to France.

In Halifax his wife Min lived with her four children, her mother-in-law, brother-in-law and his family. On the day of the explosion all the windows of the house were smashed. The family received small cuts from broken glass. The house was in disarray but in the upper hall remained a ship model of Queen Victoria's royal yacht built by John A's father unmoved by the blast and still intact.

Min Beed while out trying to find lamp oil and milk for the children, became lost in the blinding snow; the family were quite concerned as she was gone for the whole day. A man recognized her and helped her through the drifts back to Gerrish Street, her long skirt and coat heavy with ice.

Min's family, the Mulcahie's at 99 Cunard Street were slightly injured. Her mother was found unconscious on a dead wagon—her boots and coat identified by her daughter Kathleen. The woman was thought dead by those picking up bodies. She was quickly assisted to her home.

Esther Beed, daughter of George who worked at Customs House, Cheapside. Almost 3 years old at time of explosion, she has few memories of the day but remembers they were in the basement after the explosion and her aunt Min [Mary Ann Beed] became quite upset and thought it was the Germans attacking the city. Later Esther kept running to her mother telling of strange sights seen from the front storm porch, such as an injured man being piggybacked by another to

Sgt. and Min Beed with children Mary, Albert, George, and the baby Charles in a 1916 photo—a copy was taken to war. On Dec. 6, 1917 a holy picture fell over the baby's crib and protected him from harm as the windows crashed in. Charles would be lost at sea off Ireland 23 years later during the Second World War while serving in the Merchant Navy along with 6 other boys of the Brunswick Street area.

Brunswick Street and the doctors' homes there. The threat of a second explosion meant they were taken to Commons and the children received cookies from people in houses along Cunard Street.

Mary Beed age 6, daughter of John A. and Min Beed, was at Saint Patrick's Girls School on Brunswick Street. The Sisters of Charity helped her out of school; she was not hurt so was allowed to run up to the corner to her home.

Mary Beed as a young girl slept at the foot of her grandmother's bed and she recalled grandmother Bridget Beed had been at the Infirmary having an eye operation. Confirmation of this is in the Fraser Harris Report: 'A doctor reports "The morning of the disaster I was on the top floor of the Halifax Infirmary, Barrington Street. I was in the front north room dressing the eye of an elderly lady [Bridget Beed] on whom I had operated two days previously for a cataract. With me in the room were Sister Elizabeth Seton and a nurse. I had just about completed bandaging my patient when I felt a tremendous shock, the building seeming to shake as if an earthquake were in action. Sister Seton, who was standing at the bedside, said to me, 'What is that, Doctor?' I replied, 'I do not know' and made another turn of the bandage around the patient's head, when suddenly there seemed to me to be a great flash of light, followed by a roar of crashing glass, which flew all around us.

I thought the building had been struck by a shell from a submarine that had in some way worked up the harbour, and every moment I expected another shell to strike the building. I did my best to quiet my patient, who was very much excited and trying to get out of bed....I suppose five or ten minutes elapsed before numerous injured people came hurrying upstairs to the operating room. I worked for some time before I realized that the disaster was more general and that it was not only the Infirmary that was injured. I then rushed downstairs and told my chauffeur, who was at the door, to drive out to my house on Coburg Road and tell my wife I was all right."'

Medical men of the 85th on the steps of a hospital in France. Sgt. John A. Beed seated in centre of steps.

Ruins of the Glenister Family home 61 Kenny Street. Thomas Raddall a young student walked through the ruins of Richmond and came to the house of friends, the Glenisters. He thought they had been killed but discovered that the three oldest children had been in school and were unhurt. Mrs. Glenister was trapped in the wreckage of the house with her youngest child. With a broken arm and leg she was able to pull herself and the child out of the cellar to safety as the house started to burn. Like many Halifax families her husband was in the army overseas. At 53 Kenny Street the home of the Samuel Orr family, only the daughter, Barbara survived. A clear view to the narrows of the harbour can be seen in the centre right of the photo.

Bridget Beed's family, the Stokes and their in-laws, the Hinch's and the Glenister's, lived in the Northend. They lost homes, were seriously injured, were blinded and more than forty of the extended Northend family died.

Bridget's son, Sgt. John A. was one of the many men overseas who would receive telegrams telling them whether their families had died or survived in Halifax. As his family was uninjured he was to stay in Europe until 1919. His family spent the winter in the kitchen lit by oil lamps; with wood and the good parlour carpet covering windows. Permanent repairs were not undertaken until after the war, but the gas light fixtures would never be used again.

Sgt. John A. and Min Beed reunited June 15, 1919 in the garden of the Mulcahie home at 99 Cunard St. with A. A. Albert. Sgt. Beed is wearing his 85th Highlanders' uniform.

Sgt. Beed saw many wounded and dead as a medical orderly and for 'his conspicuous gallantry' received a military medal and citation. His daughter Mary would proudly receive the medal at a ceremony at Government House in 1918.

### Sisters of Charity, 321 Brunswick Street:
At age six Mary Beed remembered running home after the Sisters helped the children through broken glass at the school. Sister Julia Teresa, a teacher at Saint Patrick's Girls School made an account in 1965 of what happened at the school and convent on Brunswick Street. In part:

'On the First Thursday of every month, the General Communion Day for the girls of the parish, classes did not begin until 8:50. The floors in the school were oiled, so that during prayers, the girls knelt on their chairs, facing a large picture of the Sacred Heart, thus their backs were to the windows on the side of the room. From my place at the front of the room near the windows, I felt a slight tremor and I looked out the window and saw the chimney of Phelan's house crumble to the flat roof. Almost at the same time a loud explosion shook our building shaking us with it. The floor rocked up and down, glass from the windows blew inside the room, the wood paneling of the ceiling began to fall, with plaster from the walls. The girls screamed and ran to the door. I thought our furnace had exploded so I followed the girls to my post at the head of the stairs.... I remained at the head of the stairs somewhat stunned and bracing myself to the post of the banister as the children ran down the stairs. Several times my beads and my apron went along with them.....

Soon Father Delaney came upstairs to see if all the children were out of the building. We searched the rooms and dressing-rooms on the second floor, but found no children. Then the children returned for their coats, rubbers; etc. Father feared that the building was unsafe, so he told them to go back to the yard and we would throw all coats down to them.

As we went into the yard, we met Sister Marianita walking up the yard toward Creighton Street. When asked where she was going she replied, "To the Convent." But Sister was walking in the opposite direction. We took her to the school gate... Sister Marianita began to get faint and stumble so we practically carried her to the Convent where some Sisters cared for her.

Saint Patrick's Girls High School on Brunswick Street pre 1917.

At the gate of the Convent yard we met Sister Maria Augustine (Surette) standing with several High School girls.

Sister had no cap, a large gash in her forehead was bleeding.... One of the girls said to another girl "Oh Helen, your skirt's all wet." We took Helen into the basement of the Convent and put her into the maid's room. Suddenly Father Quinan came running down the stairs and anointed Helen. Mrs. Sullivan, an ardent worker in the Senior Children of Mary, commandeered a car on Brunswick Street and took Helen home. Her doctor removed a large piece of glass, which was within a few inches of her heart....

...Our Superior, Sister Mary Aquinas, asked the young sisters to try and clean up the house.... We donned blue aprons and sleeves and went to the refectory. All dishes were smashed, well sprinkled with pepper, salt, vinegar, mustard and sugar. So we just took the ends of the table cloths and shook the contents on the floor. With brooms we pushed the debris into piles. While doing this a sailor came running down the stairs yelling out, 'All out to the South Commons. There is danger of a second explosion'.... Sister Superior told us to get our cloaks, bonnets, rubbers and mittens and go to the Commons. Sister Superior told us to keep walking and to say the rosary. Soon groups of people were following us and praying with us.... Soldiers and sailors were hurrying around with blankets for the women and children. Priests from the Seminary and all Catholic churches were passing from group to group blessing and consoling the people....I don't recall how long we were at the Commons.... We returned to the Convent.... About one o'clock Mother Berchmans arrived on a truck and told us of the damage to the Mount and to the Sisters. Sister Superior then told Mother of the request of the Camp Hill officer [to help at the hospital]. Mother said, "By all means, let the Sisters do what they can. Sister Dominic is missing and we can't find her. (Sister Dominic was the housekeeper at St. Joseph's Convent.) If you find any of our Sisters bring them to the Infirmary."

We set out in two's—a senior sister and a junior sister, I was sent with Sister Mary Michael (neither of us know anything about "First-Aid.")

At Camp Hill hospital we saw a sight never to be forgotten: Bodies lying on the floor, some on mattresses, others on blankets, blood streaming from various parts of their bodies. Most of them were conscious...calling for help for their dear ones. Doctors and orderlies were bending over these victims trying to help them....

Camp Hill Hospital newly built for 280 beds had to accommodate 1,400 wounded. Warm bricks would be put in with patients to combat the drafts from broken windows.

We saw a lady moaning and praying so we bent down to her and asked if she as a Catholic and would she like to see a priest. Sister then said who we were. The woman then said, "Yes, I went to Holy Communion this morning and have my Child of Mary on," and she began to pull the chain around her neck. Sister asked her name and she replied; "Mrs. Stokes from St. Joseph's parish. My daughter, Kathleen, goes to St. Patrick's High School. I wonder where she is." Sister Mary Michael then said, "Kathleen is in my [class] room. We'll try to find her." All the time the woman kept her eyes closed. A Eudist priest came along and said he would anoint her. We stepped aside while Father spoke to her and then answered the prayers with Father. As Father lifted a lock of hair that had fallen over the woman's face, the scalp moved and we could see the gray matter of her brain. We gasped and so did Father. We then left her telling her we would try to find Kathleen. The air was stifling, and the odor of blood, oil, soot, sweat, and sea water nearly nauseated us.

...We thought that Kathleen might be upstairs so we made our way to the next floor. Here was a ward, the length of the building with cots in rows, possibly a hundred or more. We looked about, Sister Mary Michael looked for Kathleen, whom I did not know, while I looked for Sister Dominic with whom I had lived for two years. We found Kathleen propped up in a cot, with her leg in a cast. Sister Mary Michael talked with her while I looked about.... Suddenly a weak voice called, "O, Sister Julia Teresa, take me home, take me home." My blood froze, my breath almost stopped. Who knew me among these strangers!! I turned in the direction of the voice and stared at a figure walking toward me. The head was heavily bandaged with only one eye visible. The black cloak was caked with blood. By this time I recovered enough to answer, but the voice continued, "Don't you know me? I am Sister Dominic, take me home with you." "Of course I know you, Sister, and we'll take you to the Infirmary and our Sisters will care for you....

Downstairs we met an orderly.... I recognized him as a former pupil of mine at Oxford School. We asked if he could get us a car to take Sister Dominic to our Infirmary. He saluted and went outside and hailed a car. We were surprised to see the ground covered with snow and a strong wind blowing into drifts.

...Sister Mary Michael then decided to return to the Convent as it was getting dark and the storm seemed to be getting heavier. I don't recall how we got back to St. Patrick's Convent....

...The storm had now developed into a real blizzard and the snow blew into the rooms. Father Delaney came back to the Convent to help us. Another Sister and I helped Father to pull up the linoleum from the basement floors and Father then nailed the pieces to the window frames in the large dormitory on the third floor. I was one of the eight Sisters who slept in the dormitory. In the morning snow banks greeted us by our beds. We had to take our clothing and jump over the piles and dress in the corridor. During the night the strong wind had loosened the linoleum and the snow blew in. We thought the temperature must have been near zero. The next night we slept on mattresses in the Community Room, as the top floor was declared unsafe. We found out later that large pieces of metal had broken the corners of the roof on the harbour side of the house. . . .

. . .On the afternoon December 8, a man came to the Convent to see if any one wanted to send out any messages. I sent a message to my family that I was safe so that relieved their anxiety, as reports in the newspaper said the city was destroyed.

All schools in the Northend of the City, and also in the central part were closed. In order to draw salaries, the school authorities said that all teachers were to help all the social agencies and emergency centers in providing for the wounded, helpless and homeless. A Junior Sister and a Senior Sister were assigned to work in different areas. The Senior Sister had to make out a report of the needs and condition of the families visited each day. Sister Maria Leo and I were partners. The reports had to be sent in to a central agency where the needs were supplied. On these visits we had to listen to many sad and harrowing stories and experiences of the family. After a few days one expression seemed to be repeated so many times that we, the Junior Sisters, applied the expression to anyone who did not see our way of thinking and so should be excused. "She was cut in the head" became a by-word with us.

While our school was being repaired we shared the school days with St. Mary's Girls' School in half sessions, as there were not enough rooms for all our classes. I occupied the room called St. Anthony's hall, outside the Convent Chapel. I am sure the St. Mary's Sisters were distracted at their noon prayers—especially when I said "eighty foah" instead of eight-four.

In Halifax at noon a cannon was shot off at the Citadel to mark the official time of 12 o'clock. At St. Patrick's that shot was only heard when the wind was from the south and then sounded like a distant boom. But at St. Mary's we heard the real sound of the shot. Every day for weeks our girls jumped, screamed and ran for the door, when the cannon went off at 12 o'clock. The teachers of course experienced a shock, but we had to try not to show any exterior emotion.

The Medical Unit from Massachusetts was set up on Gottingen Street at the Admiralty House. We heard much praise from the people of the work of the doctors who served in this unit. "The Yankee" doctors brought relief and happiness to people who had broken glass in their eyes.

Our own Sister Felix lost her glasses on the day of the explosion. The previous year she had been fitted to glasses in Boston. Her lament was that now she could not see, hence could not teach. Some Sister wrote the Boston doctor and sent Sister's prescription. In a few days a box arrived with a pair of new frames and lenses with a note. The doctor was pleased and happy to send Sister the glasses and honored that he could help in a time of disaster. No bill! Sister Felix let us know on many occasions of the goodness of "my Yankee doctor". . . .'

Sister Julia Teresa (July 20, 1965)

### Myrtle MacDonald of 8 Seldon Street:

Some people think that only the Northend suffered in the explosion. Injuries also occurred in other areas of the city because of flying debris. Myrtle MacDonald was coming home from a store on Norwood Street, her mind on school. The blast happened as the 14 year old stepped inside the door of her westend family home on Seldon Street. She lost sight in her left eye from flying debris. In later life Myrtle [MacDonald] Pitcher moved to Northwood Centre in Northend Halifax.

Damage was also done to westend churches. Some claims were: J. Wesley Smith Memorial $2,000. St. Mathias $15,000. West End Baptist $4,000. Robie Street Methodist $2,000. Lutheran Church $3,000. Oxford Street Church and parsonage $9,000, the church was badly damaged, the organ ruined.

### Local Doctors did heroic job:

In some cases every room in their houses was filled with wounded persons. Many did operations both at the hospitals and in their own houses for three days, without obtaining sufficient time for sleep. Doctors provided free service until Dec. 20, 1917. Local doctors and nurses as well as private citizens saw to the most seriously wounded before outside help arrived. The Americans sent the first organized medical unit.

From the Fraser Harris Report: 'Doctor and Mrs. O'Shaughnessy—Their house on Gottingen Street was very badly damaged, and both the doctor and his wife were injured by falling woodwork. Dr. O'Shaughnessy had three ribs broken on the right side, and his right wrist badly cut. Mrs. O'Shaughnessy received a severe gash on the right arm and was cut on the chin and lips. Nevertheless, the doctor and his wife dressed the wounds of the injured continuously from a few minutes after the explosion until five p.m. on the afternoon of that day.'

A story of interest is that of Dr. Murdock Chisholm, 303 Brunswick Street; he was terribly injured on Dec. 6 and the newspapers mistakenly reported that he was dead. He read the obituary note while recovering at the Victoria General Hospital. Five sons and one daughter were serving overseas at the time of the explosion; one son was killed in battle September 1918.

### Sheppard Family of 77 Victoria Road:

As told to the author by his grandmother Gladys Sheppard [Lee], her twin Grayce Sheppard [Robinson] and their sister Charlotte Sheppard [Hartlin.]

Mr. & Mrs. Thomas Sheppard and family lived at Victoria Road, in Southend Halifax, a short walk to Point Pleasant Park and the Golf Links at Gorsebrook. The following stories are from 3 of their 7 children.

Charlotte 'Lottie' Sheppard was 20 years old and working at Moirs Chocolate Factory on Argyle Street. The explosion broke windows in the building, some thought machinery had blown up. The nerves of many girls working there were badly shaken so they gladly accepted a holiday in Maine the next year.

Charlotte was to marry Philip Hartlin. He was overseas and received a telegram stating his mother Catherine age 46, his sister Hattie age 25, and nephew Winfield age 20 months, had died at the family home on East Young Street. His sister, Mrs. Hattie Shaw was expecting and had moved home from Quinpool Road, as her husband Lieut. Alfred Shaw had sailed for overseas the week before Dec. 6. Like many of the survivors, Philip's father, Reuben, decided to rebuild away from the Northend. He built a replacement home at 83 Edinburgh Street, August 1918. A well for water was across the street.

In 1992 during the 75th Anniversary gathering at City Hall, Charlotte was to recall that her father had not put up the storm windows because of the mild December. After the explosion he was able to replace most of the broken ones with the storms. This story of 'finally getting around to it' was common to many homes in Halifax-Dartmouth.

Grayce Sheppard, age 16, was looking after children of a family in the Victoria Road area. Uninjured she took the children to join hundreds of others on the grounds of Gorsebrook Golf Links to wait until it was declared safe to return. She later moved to Massachusetts to look

The twins Grayce and Gladys in their Confirmation dresses before going to Saint Paul's Church in 1915. They are standing by a pillar on edge of Gorsebrook Golf Links on South Street. During the war Gladys and Grayce knitted socks for soldiers and sold postals to them. Grayce was very proud of the camera prize she won through selling postals.

for work, married Reginald Robinson, an American, and stayed. On visiting her in 1992 in Westboro, Massachusetts, she still clearly remembered a kind soldier giving them blankets to keep warm that day in 1917. She also recited one of the 10¢ poems that was sold shortly after the explosion.

Gladys Sheppard was the closest of the family to the explosion. A friend of the family, Bessie Acles, had invited Gladys to stay the night of December 5 on Black Street in the Northend as the lady's husband was working overnight at the new Imperial Oil Plant in Eastern Passage across the harbour. At breakfast the next morning [Dec. 6] Gladys' offer to wash up the dishes was turned aside and the two women went into the parlour to chat. Suddenly the house shook, plaster and glass shattered and the lid on the piano lifted up and flew through the window. Their initial thought was 'it was the Germans.' Sorting themselves Gladys realized she was bleeding and the blood would ruin the green corduroy suit that her mother had made for her 16th birthday just five days past.

Looking out into the neighbourhood they could see smoke, the fires that started chased them out of the house. Around them 'people bleeding and dying, it was just awful to see.' Gladys made her way to the Commons, then to the newly opened soldiers' hospital, Camp Hill, where she tried to help. Overcome by the sight of the dead and dying, she headed for home on Victoria Road to see how her family had fared. Unknown to her at the time, her mother, Selina, had walked to the Northend to search for Gladys but was turned back by soldiers at North

Some members of the Sheppard family on doorstep of 77 Victoria Road, Charlotte wearing dustcap in doorway, Mervin, George and Isabel on steps.

Street who were blocking the area to all but official search parties. It was many hours later that the family would be reunited having suffered only minor injuries.

January 29, 1918, along with other Southenders, the Sheppard family had to leave their home again as a fire broke out on the *Picton* a ship with a munitions cargo that had spot fires since December 6. Luckily that fire was controlled.

Gladys [Sheppard] Lee told her story during an interview in 1995 for the television programme, Good Morning America. She lives just around the corner from where she survived on December 6, 1917.

St. George's Rector H. W. Cunningham views ruined organ.

Police (military) headquarters in the Naval Dockyard.

## Hinch and Stokes Family, Richmond District:

Of the many affected by the explosion, the Hinch and Stokes families present a sad picture of the results. Forty plus members of the extended family were killed, three were completely blinded, two lost sight in one eye and one lost a leg. Here is a record of what happened to some:

Joseph Hinch, 66 Veith Street, and ten children killed. Four were buried in one box in Mount Olivet Cemetery. His wife was the lone survivor of the immediate family.

Edward Hinch was on the train stopped because of the message sent by Vincent Coleman and all on board were saved. Edward's wife was safe, his brother Fred was missing, later found dead, as was his son, Arthur.

John Hinch, brother of Edward, of 21 Acadia Street lost one eye while working in rail yards but survived the tidal wave. His wife, Mary and son, Laurie, blown out of the house survived uninjured. His other son, Thomas, watching the fire from the dining room was blinded. He

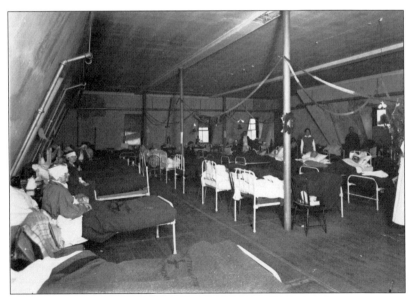

later graduated from Dalhousie University, with tutoring by Barbara Orr, a local girl who lost many of her family.

Mary Hinch's mother, Mrs. Margaret Stokes, 25 Acadia Street, survived blinded and badly scarred. Husband, John Sr., [Bridget Beed's brother] a carpenter at CGR, age 48 and son, John Jr., a clerk at Montreal News Co. were killed. Son, Allan Stokes, was blinded. He also graduated from university with tutoring provided by Barbara Orr. The four daughters survived though Kathleen lost her leg, Agnes lost an eye and Frances was badly cut. Helen was the only one uninjured.

William Hinch of 37 Young Street was killed.

David Hinch Sr., 18 Richmond Street, a boiler maker reached home and found that it had first collapsed then burned to ground. In the ruins were his wife, Louise, and children, John 11 years, Catherine 11 months, Harold 17 years—all dead. Leo Hinch 16 years, messenger boy for Canadian Press was safe.

David Hinch Jr., 24 Richmond Street, rushed home to find wife, Isabelle, cut in two and 2 year old son, missing [later listed as body #1278].

As with all survivors, life had to go on for David Jr.:

From Halifax newspapers of Jan. 4, 1918: 'For the Homeless—The building 112 Hollis Street known as the Theakstone Apartments has been taken over by the Relief Committee and will be used as permanent living quarters. The building is being put in good condition and when completed will have room for twenty-five families without crowding. The shelter will be run by David Hinch Jr. who lost his family in the explosion and nearly all his relatives. Mr. Hinch is acquainted with all the destitute families of Richmond and his appointment as head of the shelter is a popular one.'

**Saint Mary's College, Windsor Street, housed many injured. Rooms were decorated for Christmas.**

A view looking southeast in the Richmond District.

# The Gazette.

WEATHER FORECAST:
FAIR; DECIDEDLY COLD

TEMPERATURE YESTERDAY
Max. 18 above; min. 5 above

VOL. CXLVI. NO. 293          MONTREAL, FRIDAY, DECEMBER 7, 1917 —TWENTY-TWO PAGES          PRICE TWO CENTS

## Halifax Disaster Death List Estimated At 2000
## Munition Ship Blew Up, Laying North End In Ruins

### BELGIAN RELIEF SHIP GORED HULL
### OF EXPLOSIVE-LADEN FRENCH CRAFT

Damaged Vessel Caught Fire---25 Minutes Later Terrific Con-
vulsion Spread Death, Injury and Destruction Over Wide
Area---Property Loss Will Reach Millions, Every Structure in the City Being Shaken ---One in Each Two Surviving Residents Injured --- Temporary Morgues and
Hospitals Improvised ---Relief Rushed to Stricken City
from Many Points in Canada and United States.

### RISKY SALIENT ABANDONED BY BYNG'S FORCES

18 Mile Arc Becomes 10-Mile
Straight Line

PLANS CAREFULLY LAID

Germans Apparently Knew Nothing of Movement
Until Next Day

### 6 GOTHAS OF 25 REACH LONDON; 2 REMAIN THERE

Latest Air Raid Was Determined
But Futile

7 DEATHS ARE REPORTED

Two Hostile Machines Downed
and Crews Captured
Alive

### HUN LOSSES IN ATTACK BEYOND EXAGGERATION

Were Extraordinarily Great —
Ground Still With Corpses

EXPECT SECOND EFFORT

More Live Masses Will Be
Pushed Forward at
Any Moment

### HOSTILITIES ARE SUSPENDED FOR TEN DAYS

Agreement Between Teutonic
Allies and Russians

FIXED FOR FRIDAY NOON

Period Will Be Utilized to
Conclude Armistice
Negotiations

---

# The Gazette.

WEATHER FORECAST:
FAIR AND COLD

TEMPERATURE YESTERDAY
Max. 20 above; min. 10 above

VOL. CXLVI. NO. 295          MONTREAL, MONDAY, DECEMBER 10, 1917 —TWENTY PAGES          PRICE TWO CENTS

## Elements Still Scourge Desolated City of Halifax
## 1050 Bodies at Morgues; All Germans Being Arrested

### DELUGE HINDERS SEARCH OF DEBRIS;
### GOVERNMENT GIVES MILLION TO RELIEF

Under Military Orders, Police Begin Roundup of All German
Residents---Enquiry Begins Tuesday Before Admiralty
Judge---Survivors of Colliding Ships Under Arrest---Pro-
posal to Return Liberal and Unionist By Acclamation---
Non-Residents Asked to Leave Because of Food Short-
age---Call for Workers and Supplies---Stories of Heroism
Among Soldiers and Seamen---Death Estimate Still 2,000

### EVIL SPELL OF POISON FOREST IS LIFTED NOW

Only One British Casualty in Liberation and
Evacuating Bourlon Wood

ENEMY LOST HEAVILY

Great Relief for Britons as
Leave Such a Place

### COSSACK CHIEFS DECLARE WAR ON THE REVOLUTION

Esthonian and Livonia Rise Re-
volt in One Country

CIVIL WAR STARTED

Bolsheviki Orders Immediate
Attack Bridgehead

### INCREDIBLE HAPPENINGS INCIDENT TO DISASTER

Man Blown Half Mile But Escapes Death
---Babies Found Uninjured in Debris
---City Clocks Stopped at 9.05 ---
Heroic Operator Tried to Give Warn-
ing---Newspapers Resume Publica-
tion---Ship Afire Yesterday Caused
Alarm---Brave Work By Rescuers

Front pages from *The Gazette*, Montreal, December 1917.

Chapter 5

# The Dominion of Canada Unites

*'From many a sister city*
*Their help we did obtain*
*And from many a town and hamlet*
*O'er Canada's broad domain*

*We thank those true Canadians*
*Who answered to the call*
*And sent us needed aid that day.*
*We thank them one and all.'*

Verses from *Record of Halifax Explosion* by Clark Hall

Men surveying damage to Rope Works, Windmill Road, Dartmouth.

The Dominion of Canada celebrated 50 years as a nation in July 1917. [9 provinces and 2 territories, as Newfoundland did not join until 1949] The young nation united from sea to sea as offers of help were made to ease the suffering from what is still Canada's largest disaster—wartime or peacetime. The federal government provided the major portion of the estimated $35 million dollars needed to rebuild the city and to look after the survivors.

The community nearest the disaster site on the edge of Halifax was a black settlement known as Africville. Africville received less damage from the blast because of its shielded position overlooking Bedford Basin. The community rallied to help the injured who were coming down the railway line from Richmond.

Due to the amount of gunpowder, ash and soot that rained down on the city many dead and injured were thought to be black.

Sister Julia Teresa, a teacher living at Saint Patrick's Convent, Brunswick Street wrote in her remembrance of the explosion. 'A large truck passed by with blood dripping from it just as water dripped from 'ice carts'... Bodies... all black protruding in all directions. I concluded that these people came from Africville, a small Negro settlement just outside Halifax near Fairview.'

Archibald MacMechan, the official historian of the disaster wrote of the blast 'It blackened faces and bodies of all it fell on, in some cases making it impossible to distinguish white persons from negroes.'

Dr. Fraser Harris would observe 'at first many of the patients from the burning district were so blackened by the soot as to be even after critical examination mistaken for negroes.'

Another story associated with the oily tar that hit the city can now be looked on with some amusement. It is still told that while working among those brought to the gymnasium of Mount Saint Vincent Academy in Rockingham, a Sister of Charity bent down to wipe the face of an injured black man. As she took away the cloth Sister almost fainted as his cheek had turned white. Further tending revealed that he was a white person and she had caused no injury.

In fact only ten persons of African descent are listed as killed by the explosion. This includes body #349, James Allison of Africville age 40 who like others had stopped to watch the fire on the way to work. He was identified at the Chebucto School mortuary by the Reverend Moses Puryear, minister of Cornwallis Street Baptist Church.

**Train leaving for Truro with injured survivors.**

The first Nova Scotia communities to respond were located on the railway lines. Bridgewater men gathered the bodies. Windsor women provided lunches of hot soup for those on their way to Halifax to help.

Trains were also used to take the injured out of Halifax as noted in this story of Dec. 18, 1917, in the *Halifax Herald*:

'Provincial Help—First Train to Truro

(Dr.) Avery DeWitt of Wolfville, who happened to be on the early morning D.A.R. train for Halifax, was met at Rockingham by Mr. Graham, the general manager of the Railway and told of the terrible catastrophe. Dr. DeWitt was put on a shunter and taken into Richmond at express speed. The engine driver, who had nothing on but his shirt and trousers and who was badly cut and covered with dirt, refused to give up his place to anyone else, saying, "All my people were killed before my eyes. I have nobody left; I gave my clothes to cover a wounded child; so that all I can do now is to help others."

At Richmond it did not, unfortunately, take long to fill the train with the injured and dying, with whom Dr. DeWitt and a few unwounded passengers travelled in the direction of Truro. At Windsor Junction, Dr. George DeWitt of Wolfville and Nurse Nellie DeWitt, father and sister respectively of Major DeWitt, boarded the train.

Arriving in Truro, the DeWitts worked without food or rest all the remainder of December 6th and during the following night in the emergency hospitals, which had been arranged on very short notice. Truro converted her courthouse, academy and fire hall to hospitals. Everybody in Truro turned out to help and hundreds of women and men continued to work day and night.'

Truro only 60 miles from Halifax had felt the explosion. Windows and walls had shaken, china fell from cupboards. One woman reported her baby carriage had jumped from her hands and overturned. Horses with wagons rushed about wildly in the streets.

The town was quickly ready for the Halifax injured after meetings presided over by Colonel John Stanfield. A citizen's relief committee organized households into preparing food boxes to be taken to Halifax along with doctors, nurses and 200 men. Many citizens took refugees

Notices appeared in newspapers to ask that only essential people stay in town. This hotel at Gottingen and Almon Streets would not be ready to receive guests for months.

into their homes. By December 7th, 400 destitute were in Truro, many received new clothes, there were ten deaths among the wounded. On December 19 Truro sent $7,000 to Halifax for relief work.

New Glasgow was another town that received wounded from Halifax and sent volunteers to help in relief work. A hospital was set up in the West Side School. A hundred patients were treated, some of them sent from the American hospital ship, *Old Colony*. On discharge from the hospital, the town made sure each person received a new set of clothes. With only twenty-nine patients left in the school building they were moved to the Aberdeen hospital—the townspeople made it clear they would care for them as long as they had need. The women of the town, under Superintendent Miss Sinclair, were assisted in their work by volunteers and supplies from neighbouring communities. Trenton, Stellarton and Westville citizens contributed beds, bedding, linen, surgical supplies and food.

Many towns prepared to receive people from Halifax but due to bad weather the injured remained in Halifax. With the influx of medical personnel from the United States and Canada, the temporary hospitals and clinics in the city could look after all who sought help.

Middleton was one such town that prepared to take the injured. They were told to prepare for fifty children who did not arrive. Halifax decided to look after all the children in hopes that family members might be found. Middleton with a population of a few hundred sent through their Red Cross '75 quilts, 39 blankets, 12 pillows, 60 women's' coats, suits for men and women, undergarments suitable for men, women, children and money for subscribing to relief fund.' This, and other news items, were recorded in the weekly issue of the town paper *The Outlook*. One reason Halifax could cope with the homeless was recorded in the newspaper. People who were working in Halifax returned home for the winter taking with them others who had lost their homes. So the burden of housing was spread across the province.

*The Outlook* Dec. 1917—Jan. 1918 gives a line or two to allow readers a glimpse of what was happening. Due to a small readership and costs, the paper contained no pictures. The reports included:

'People with little offered room to many, some were so dazed they would not leave their ruined homes as they waited for those who would not return.'

'4 trains sent from Moncton on Dec. 6.' '2 doctors motored from Lunenburg.' 'Bodies piled up like cordwood.' '50,000 blankets required.'

'Chas. B. McIntyre of Aylesford died Sunday Dec. 9 from injuries of Thursday, age 54, left wife and daughter.'

'Guy Ferguson returns to Port George home safe from Halifax Dockyards.'

'Fred Moxon lost wife, 4 children, father and mother.'

'450 soldiers invalided to Halifax week before explosion help in the relief work.'

'Bridgetown Town Council votes $500. T.B. Chipman started private fund with $100.'

'Toronto Train with supplies and 25 nurses sent.'

'DEC 7 New York several trains of New York Central Railway speeding to Halifax with men and supplies.'

'DEC 10 Providence, Rhode Island Journal reported start of fund. Train sent with personnel and supplies to care for 500 injured.' 'Penobscot County Maine sent 10,000 blankets, 1,000 cots, medical men, nurses.' 'The Delaware and Hudson Railway sent load of lumber and clothing.'

'SS CALVIN AUSTIN from Boston brought blankets, cots, clothes and 1100 gallons of milk.' [The ship put in at Yarmouth due to storm conditions, so much needed milk could be sent by train.]

'DEC 13 SS NORTHLAND brought relief cargo from Massachusetts valued at $150,000.'

'Dominion Atlantic Railway offers free transportation of relief supplies. Free train passes for any wanting to leave Halifax from all railways.'

Provincial help came from many sources as a review of Relief Committee files at the Public Archives of Nova Scotia reveals:

Wolfville offered to take 100 injured and nurses. Kentville could take 200 people. Bridgewater offered to take in 25 to 100 people. Mr. CN McIntyre of McNair's Lake, Richmond County offered to organize farmers to send produce to Halifax. Donation from Inverness Catholic Congregation, $550.00. Western Union offered large store houses on Cable Wharf for shelter. Nova Scotia Reserve Battalion sends $200 for dependants of men overseas.

From across the Dominion of Canada offers of help quickly arrived. Notables of Canadian society made large contributions. The Premier of the Dominion of Canada [now referred to as the Prime Minister], Sir Robert Borden, offered the help of the Dominion and referred with particular feeling to the prompt way 'our United States friends responded.'

—Mrs. Bell, wife of inventor Alexander Graham Bell, organized the work of the ladies of Baddeck, Cape Breton, these supplies were sent by boat to Halifax. Mr. Bell sent his associate, Casey Baldwin, to Halifax

Train passing demolished buildings in Richmond District, SS *Imo* on opposite shore. From newspapers: 'approaching trains Dec. 6 turned baggage cars into first aid centres.' Railway men were complimented on their efforts to keep trains moving even during blizzards of snow. Conductors did their best to comfort the injured and displaced, many of them Halifax railway families devastated by the explosion.

and Truro to investigate scientific aspects of the explosion. They were most interested in the 'wave' that set the bells ringing in Truro. The private journal of Archibald MacMechan, official historian of the disaster, records Baldwin's visit for more practical reasons: 'DEC 14 Baldwin from Baddeck came to see us late last night at Dalhousie, brought 3 carpenters who made further repairs.'

—Lord Thomas Shaughnessey, President., Canadian Pacific Railway and chairman of Victory Loan Organization offered services of Victory Loan Staff from Quebec. He sent a train load of boots, bedding and glass as his personal contribution.

### At the home of the Foster's in Princeport:

Pauline [Foster] Carter recalls her parents' experience in Princeport, Colchester County on the morning of December 6, 1917. Clarence and Gertrude Foster were going about their chores—Gertrude working in the house and Clarence outside milling grain with an engine powered machine. Feeling a tremendous rumble, they each thought something catastrophic had happened to the other. They ran to each other—discovering that neither was harmed. Perplexed, they would not learn until later of the source of the tremendous rumble that shattered a second storey window. The explosion in Halifax Harbour some 50 miles south was the cause of their alarming experience. Clarence preserved the 'explosion' window as a curiosity piece by applying a new sheet of glass over the broken one.

—Lady Lillian Beck, a noted equestrian, London, Ontario sent by train a carload of new children's clothing.

—Sir Thomas White, Finance Minister of the Dominion of Canada agreed all relief funds would go directly to the accounts in Halifax.

—Chebucto Chapter, Daughters of Empire offered to cook as needed at Union Jack Club. Mrs. William Dennis announced other chapters of Daughters of the Empire, Women's Council and Red Cross ready!

—Price Waterhouse & Co. rendered free accounting services to the relief committees until Dec 31, 1917.

—L. M. Montgomery, the author, recorded in her diary on December 7 what she had learned of the explosion the day before. Coming out of the Eaton's store in Toronto she saw newspapers headlined 'Halifax disaster' and thought it was a fake story or a ship sunk named 'Halifax.' She realized after reading the story that she had been travelling on the tram for twenty minutes overcome by the news. As she had lived in Halifax as a student of Dalhousie College, and as a newspaper reporter, she was concerned for her many friends. Like other Canadians she responded with a donation.

Telegrams offering help arrived as in this one from Lady Borden, wife of Sir Robert Borden, Premier of Canada to Mrs. Grant, wife of the Lieutenant Governor of Nova Scotia:

Lady Borden, Ottawa
'To Mrs. Grant,
Government House, Halifax
Dec. 7th 1917
Can we help with Red Cross Hospital Supplies, such as pajamas, socks, hospital shirts, some sheets and quilts.
Laura Borden.'

Mrs. Grant replied that the supplies would be most welcome.

Telegrams were sent to thank donors:

Dec. 13th 1917

Reply to Miss Margaret L. Evans, President Red Cross Society, Shediac, N.B.

'Appreciate very much your sending oysters which have been distributed as per your letter. I am sure the poor sick will enjoy the treat very much indeed.

Lieut. Col. F. McKelvey Bell. Chairman Medical Relief Committee'

December 17th 1917

Reply to Mr. Thos. Gillespie & Co. Montreal.

'Very many thanks for your kind gift of ten cases of brandy for use of the sufferers in the Halifax Disaster. Mr. Bauld has handed this over to the Medical Services and the Medical Relief Committee thanks you on behalf of the citizens of Halifax.

T. McKelvey Bell, Lieut.-Col. Chairman Medical Relief Committee'

Funds came in from all 9 provinces:

Sir Robert Borden [Premier of Dominion of Canada] and Lady Borden $1,000.00

Province of Ontario, 100,000.00

Chief of Police Fund, Verdun, Quebec, 150.00

Winnipeg Grain Exchange, 5,000.00

Quebec Friends, Quebec, 10,000.

Sherwin Williams Co. of Canada, Toronto, 1,000.00

St. James Cathedral Sunday School, Toronto, (instead of their Christmas sweets) 9.00

Employees, Lyall Shipbuilding Co., Vancouver, 1,100.00

Lady clerks, head office Royal Bank, Montreal, 15.00

Midland Church, S. Norton, N.B. in lieu of Christmas Treats, 40.00

Citizens of Portage Laprairie, 500.00

Citizens of Preston, Manitoba, 4th donation, 86.50

Honourable James Dunsmuir, Victoria BC, 500.00

## The work of Sir John Eaton:

The Relief Committee voted Sir John Eaton an expression of gratitude: 'upon hearing of disaster engaged a special train, loaded it with clothing and other supplies and with a large staff came himself to Halifax and for more than a week working day and night directed the distribution of his generous and humane gift.'

From Halifax newspapers: 'Sir John Eaton left Windsor, N.S. for Toronto. After bringing his three carloads of much needed and welcome relief supplies to Halifax Sir John paid a visit to the wounded and the homeless who were taken to Windsor after the disaster. At the Baptist Church hall he opened up a great stock of comforts and necessities which were liberally distributed.' Shipment of goods was worth $66,000.

Sir John insisted that Toronto newspapers not cover his trip as he wanted no publicity from others' misery. Each of the seventeen managers received on returning to Toronto, a silver pin inscribed with 'E. W. S.' for Eaton's Welfare Service. On the back of the pin were the words 'Halifax Relief.'

From 'Relief Fund Column' in Halifax newspapers in order of listing:
  'A little girl $ .03
  Province of British Columbia, 50,000.00'

Goods were also sent::
  Waterloo Mennonite Charity Circle, bedding and canned goods
  Vancouver Red Cross, 17 cases blankets 98 cases heavy overcoats.
  Canadian Red Cross, Quebec City, carload stoves, sashes, etc.
  J.D. Irving, Buctouche, New Brunswick, 1 box chickens, 1 box pork, 1 quarter beef.
  Mayor of Quebec, 2 cars of mattresses
Around Nova Scotia people prepared packages for Halifax. Others retold how they first knew of the disaster. Some thought they 'heard' thunder but later they learned of the explosion and realized that they had felt the earth tremor.

Catherine Agatha Pellerine [Brousseau Deschenes]: Many miles from Halifax along the Eastern Shore of Nova Scotia. At a small school house on a hill a little girl again late for class is chastised by the teacher for throwing something against the building. A child of 9 would especially remember being blamed for something she did not do. The day was Dec. 6, 1917 and Port Felix was one of the many Maritime communities that felt or 'heard' the explosion from Halifax. Through the years Catherine would often recount how she was blamed for 'hitting the school.'

Marion Hushard [Ceretto]: The girls in Our Lady of the Assumption Convent School in Arichat heard the rattling of dishes and shaking of pictures on the morning of Dec. 6. Some thought it was a thunderstorm. Later in the day news arrived of the destruction in Halifax. Marion, a boarding student from Canso, remembered how they were to feel sorry for one of the girls from Halifax even though they were not sure why. Marion married and taught school in Halifax. For a time she lived in the rebuilt Hydrostone district.

Fred Locke and his brothers Norman and Harold on the lawn of family home in Amherst. They packed boxes for Halifax.

Fred Locke: For the boys and girls of Amherst, N.S. at the border of New Brunswick there was great excitement being sent home from school to gather supplies for the relief of Halifax. Men of the Amherst Fire Brigade joined the train bringing volunteers for Halifax. The extra whistles would be noticed for weeks as trains transporting relief supplies would rumble along the line into Nova Scotia.

Later Fred would marry Marion Hushard's sister Agnes and they would live in Halifax. He worked in Halifax as a city electrician.

More than 50 Nova Scotia communities received for burial the bodies of victims of the Halifax Disaster. In Middleton *The Outlook* reported that L.H. Tupper had left for Halifax to look for Mr. and Mrs. George Tupper. The Tupper's of North Kingston had gone to Halifax to seek medical advice. They were staying on Veith Street. Having not found their bodies, a memorial service was held and attended by their 5 young children. In Halifax newspapers, January 3, 1918, appeared the notice: 'To be added to the list of the dead are Mrs. Odessa Lavers [age 60] 75 Veith Street [corner Richmond Street] her son Everett Lavers [age 21] 9 Black Street and two friends from Kingston, Kings County Mr. and Mrs. G.E. Tupper who were visiting Mrs. Lavers.'

In *The Outlook*: 'Mr. George Tupper's body identified Friday last [Jan. 20, 1918] and taken home for burial.'

And recorded in the Mortuary records in Halifax:

'#162—M 42 George Edward Tupper visiting 75 Veith Street identified by L.H. Tupper Buried Fairview Cemetery later removed to North Kingston.' Mrs. Lydia Jane Tupper age 38 was never found.

## Chebucto School Mortuary:

There were hundreds of remains of the dead that needed to be identified. All local undertakers' rooms were filled so a mortuary was opened on Chebucto Road at the school. The last time a large mortuary had been required was five years previous when the victims of the Titanic were brought to Halifax. Mr. Barnstead of the mortuary committee recorded in his minutes thanks to the embalmers from Toronto and Kitchener, Ontario who helped set up a system of identification made especially difficult when dealing with burnt remains. Each body was given a number. Comments noted who identified them and where burial took place. A look at the file reveals a town busy with the war effort. A cross section of Halifax society was found amongst the dead:

#10—Lt. Harold Balcom age 26, Baptist, of Wellington Barracks Composite Battalion identified by Major J.E. Morse

#830—Harris Boutilier 23 years, of 340 Oxford Street, buried Fairview Cemetery identified by father John Boutilier

#837—Rodney Burnett 27 years, HMCS *Niobe* buried St. John Cemetery

#60—Hugh Henry age 29, HMCS *Niobe*, sent to Toronto for burial.

# 134—John W. Morash 33yrs, of Beverly, Massachusetts

#813—Andrew Peterson 23 yrs, American Schooner *Sawyer Bios*, buried Fairview Cemetery.

#452—Gerald Woody age 10, RC, of Bland Street identified by Albert Woody father.

#252—Private A. Roscoe 'D' Company effects still here.

#1233—Pt Alex Thompson Fyfe, 22 years, of The Armouries, buried Fort Massey Cemetery, mother 509 West 10th Street, New York.

#1267—James Williams, 44, of Jly Moorhaut Ernis hoar, Zuay, Wales, buried Fairview Cemetery.

#811—Oscar Karlstroni Coal Trimmer, *Imo*, of Sweden, buried Fairview Cemetery.

#812—Johannes Kirsenboom Carpenter, *Imo*, of Holland, buried Fairview Cemetery.

#814—R.A. Inerson Chief officer, *Imo*, of Tonshery, Norway, buried Fairview Cemetery.

#851—Vincent Coleman wireless operator, age 42, of 31 Russell Street, buried Mount Olivet Cemetery.

#852—Edward Patrick Condon 60 years, Chief, Central Fire Station, Brunswick Street, buried Holy Cross Cemetery.

#1115—Alex Moffat, 9 months, of Windsor Street, buried Petawawa Ontario.

#1123—Mary Murphy Lee, 29 years, of Albert and Kenny Streets. John Francis Lee, 4 months, buried with mother Holy Cross Cemetery.

#1134—D. Campbell, age 19, of Battersly Barre, England, buried Fairview Cemetery.

—Matteo Cecconi, 24, RC, of 69 Duke Street, stevedore, unloading SS *Picton* [supporting family in Italy] buried Mount Olivet Cemetery.

#1469—S. Bosher, of Penarth, Wales , Cook , SS *Picton*

—Hans Hermanson, 18, of Christiania, Norway, SS *Hovland* in Drydock.

#1310—Yves Guegunover, SS *Mont Blanc,* (only crew member killed by explosion.) buried Dartmouth.

#759—Margaret Sutherland, 80, of the Old Ladies Home, buried Camp Hill Cemetery.

#761—Jessie Eager, 76, of the Old Ladies Home, buried Camp Hill Cemetery.

#763—Annie Redmond, 53, corner Preston & Jubilee, buried Mount Olivet, Halifax.

Chebucto School Mortuary, showing the bodies of the explosion victims.

A view of Chebucto School where the basement was used as a mortuary.

#180—Pontleon Lemieux, 27, 2nd Engineer, SS *Musquash,* buried Levis, Quebec.

#413—John Johnson, 25, ship MT *Curaca,* of Manila, Philippine Islands.

#437—Haakon Fron, 47, Captain SS *Imo,* of Sandleford, Norway. Embalmed and sent to Norway.

#738-39-40 Hansen David Howe, 2 months, Mildred M. Howe, 4 years, Mrs. Mildred Howe, 22 years, all of Kentville NS, identified by Pte Hanson Howe.

Remains were brought to the mortuary in old tin scuttles, pails, bath tubs and wheelbarrows. The letter 'c' designated a child.

One entry in the record book reads '#525, 526c, 527c, 528c, 529c charred remains 5 bodies one family bought in wooden box marked Richmond Printing Company.'

The military played a large part in the response to the Halifax disaster. Admiral Chambers, the Royal Navy Port Convoy Officer witnessed the rising cloud over the Richmond District from the grounds of Royal Artillery Park on Sackville Street. He immediately organized surveys of damage to the ships in the harbour. On December 6, 1917, there were more than 60 vessels in the harbour with thousands of people on board. While waiting convoy or repairs personnel were not allowed off ship. This saved many lives as ships in the Bedford Basin were not hit directly by the blast. This included the White Star liner *Olympic,* [sister ship to the *Titanic*] that was carrying 5,000 Chinese workers enroute to Europe.

Those at the Richmond Piers 6, 7, 8 were not so lucky. The greenish grey harbour water would fill from shore to shore with debris, bodies and overturned boats including the Northend ferry. The ferry captain, Mr. Duggan, was found alive under the overturned boat on the Dartmouth shore. His parents were killed. His brother's family were safe except for a 3 week old baby lost to the fire that destroyed the house. The main harbour ferry was safe despite the tidal wave caused by the blast. The force of the tidal wave washed the tug *Hilford* up onto the pier. The tugs, *Musquash, Merrimac, Weatherspoon* and *Douglas H. Thomas* were severely damaged as was the river collier *J.A. McKee.*

The SS *Curaca* was swept from the Piers across to where the Indian Community of Turtle Grove was destroyed. The Captain of the ship had to identify many of the 57 dead of his crew.

The SS *Picton* was being unloaded of food and munitions cargo so that repairs could be undertaken. Seventy men working the ship died as they tried to cover the 1500 tons of shells below decks to protect the cargo from the *Mont Blanc* fire.

The SS *Hovland* was in dry dock undergoing refit. Five of the crew were killed. Of the 235 drydock workers 120 were killed, those saved were working under the ship in the dock.

The SS *Colonne*, awaiting horses was heavily damaged with 37 men killed. The SS *Middleton Castle*, merchant ship lost its funnels. The *Ragus* [sugar backwards] a new steamer for the Sugar Refinery was destroyed as was the ocean going tug *Stella Maris*.

The three masted square rigged ship *Sophie* from Norway was damaged and the schooner *St. Bernard* destroyed. Damage was also done the HMCS *Niobe*, HMCS *Margaret* and HMS *Highflyer*, all of which lost crew.

Other ships were damaged and days of storms played havoc with repairs. Some ships were pressed into service for relief efforts such as the armed Merchant Cruiser HMS *Changuinola*. The Furness Liner *Kanawh*a at pier became a shelter as did the Cable Wharf. The USS *Old Colony* where Captain Barrett would set up two operating rooms under the direction of Surgeon F.C. Patterson took 150 of the city's injured.

Communities across the country recorded the loss of their citizens as in this story carried in Halifax and Saint John newspapers:

*Halifax Herald*:

'The Sad Fate of Popular Officer Lieut. F.J. Howley Who Was Killed by the Explosion Won Promotion on the Battlefield in France.'

To go through some of the biggest battles on the western front, and escape with slight wounds, only to be killed in the Halifax explosion on December 6th, was the fate of Lieutenant F.J. Howley of the Canadian Engineers. Lieut. Howley was for many years the leading spirit of Association football in Nova Scotia, and acted on several occasions as chief adviser of the local teams. All those with soccer troubles rushed to Mr. Howley, who always managed to straighten them out. He was

## The effects of Halifax explosion were far reaching:

Many times we hear of how local people were changed by the explosion. August 1995 a passenger on a tour bus stated the explosion affected her early life in Ontario. Her story: 'Father was in the Army destined for overseas. However, he arrived in Halifax just after the explosion and was assigned to work on cleaning detail. This lasted until the next year. The war ended and he never served overseas. He returned to his wife and had a family. He died while we children were very young. As he was not an overseas veteran there was no pension monies for the family to receive. The family had a difficult time and mother always blamed it on the Halifax Explosion.' This story was recalled to the author in the same area that was destroyed by the explosion.

**Soldiers searching ruins.**

also for four years secretary of the Nova Scotia Football Association and in 1913 wrote a book on "Soccer Football, It's Growth and Origin in Halifax". Mr. Howley left Halifax with the rank of an N.C.O., but by gallant work won promotion on the battlefield, returning to this city as a lieutenant. The death of "Joe" Howley not only took from us a true sportsman but a gentleman and hero.'

The *St. John Telegram* [New Brunswick]

'William Russell arrived home on Sunday from Halifax where he had been looking after the remains of his brother-in-law, Lt. F.J. Howley and his wife and child. In company with Captain H.J. Knight of No. 3 Black Street Halifax who was a brother of Mrs. Howley.

Lt. Howley and family lost their lives December 6 in the Halifax disaster. Lt. Howley went overseas on January 1, 1915 with the Halifax and Dalhousie Red Cross Unit a sergeant and was promoted and transferred to the 26th reserve. He was at his home 3 Albert Street Halifax on 3 months furlough and was to return to front after Christmas.'

## How ordinary Canadians responded:

The pages of the *Calgary Daily Herald* from Dec. 6 to Dec. 24 1917 reveals Calgary's plan of action for the Halifax relief effort. Due to the 3 hour time difference, news appeared on Thursday, December 6 the actual day of the explosion. Reports of the disaster appeared daily and photographs of the destruction were published.

The front page of the *Calgary Daily Herald* of December 6, 1917, showed a postcard view of the city from the Citadel and headline '1200 dead in Halifax' followed by a story that a French munitions ship and a Norwegian boat had collided.

A side story titled 'Many Halifax People Live in This City' explained the newspaper office was inundated with telephone calls all day by people wanting news of Halifax. Inside pages reported messages received from various cities including Boston and Washington. Governor McCall's offer of help was published in Calgary before it had been received in Halifax due to the destruction of telegraph wires by the explosion.

Other *Calgary Daily Herald* stories:

Friday December 7: Due to distance it was thought by Mayor M. Costello of Calgary that sending money would be useful 'always a great help if given quickly' and 'that other cities in the Dominion would come forward and Calgary would certainly prove as generous hearted as any of them.' Inside headlines reported: 'All Rescue Work at a Standstill in Howling Blizzard' 'Word received late tonight that the Massachusetts relief train had been stalled in snowdrift' 'Sir James Akins, Lieut. Governor of Manitoba tonight sent a message to lieut. governor of Nova Scotia expressing Manitoba's sympathy'

Saturday December 8 'Injured dying in Snowbound Trains' 'Many Navy Men Killed Halifax lists Disclose' [Some sailors were listed with next of kin unknown]

Monday December 10 '25000 without Homes in Blizzard Storm'

Wednesday December 12 'Calgary's Quota to Halifax Relief Fund to be $30,000' 'Patrick Burns Co. and Hudson's Bay Company each give $10,000. Employees of P. Burns Company volunteered $600. Calgary Rotary Club donated $500' 'Headquarters for the Halifax Relief Committee will be old bar at Palliser Hotel Calgary.'

Mayor Costello suggested that as Winnipeg and Vancouver had each voted $25,000 and Saskatoon $5,000 Calgary should send at least $10,000 and he thought that 'the city could just as well afford $15,000 as $10,000.' So $15,000 was recommended to Council as the City Hall contribution. One commissioner suggested waiting to see what the business community would do but the Mayor suggested the money was needed immediately.

Friday December 14 'A Tag day is organized.' 'All Women's Organizations in Calgary are being asked to help.' 'White badges will read Halifax Help'

Monday December 17 'Quota for Southern Alberta Has Been Placed at $262,000' 'Alberta provincial government to cover cost of clerical staff at Palliser Hotel' 'The Musicians Union will hold a masquerade ball tomorrow with proceeds to Halifax' And a story to stir the readers: 'Returned Veterans are giving to fund, subscriptions received from boys at the Frank Sanitorium and the Ogden Home. These boys have done their bit in France but they know what the suffering is in the eastern city and when they have the chance to relieve any of this they are only too willing to do so.'

Thursday December 20 'Canvassers are Amply Rewarded for Efforts on Second Day' 'School Children are Donating Generously' From the donation columns: Alberta Pacific Grain Company, $1,500.00, APGC Employees, 156.00, Pantages Theatre employees, 12.00, Alaska Western Bedding Co., 35.50, Other Contributors; Bishop J T McNally, [who would later become Archbishop of Halifax] Barber Ellis Davis Ltd., Calgary Lodge AF AM, Rubin Hebrew School, St. Paul's Presbyterian, Revelstoke Sawmill Co., Ford Motor Co., Great Northern Insurance Co., Alberta Cattlemen, Ottis Fenson Elevator Co., United Farmers, United Grain Growers.

Monday, December 24 'Calgary Closes Halifax Relief Fund at $45,208' 'Women's Organizations netted $3,704.25 which is a record for tag days in City of Calgary.'

As in many Canadian communities, Calgary's citizens exceeded fundraising targets. The same generosity was also exercised across the border; citizens of Uncle Sam opened their hearts and pocketbooks in response to the Halifax disaster.

The appeal notice of December 10th and the thank you notice of December 11th in *The Gazette*, Montreal , illustrates the quick response to the relief effort.

**Survivors would write of their experiences to friends and family:**

At the Archives of Ontario in a collection of letters of Miss Mary Leslie, Leaksdale, Ontario, is correspondence from Cecilia Byng Clarke of 'Brooklands' which was on Pleasant Street, Dartmouth. One of the letters was on paper bordered in black as there is mention of a deceased resident of Ontario however Cecilia first describes her experiences with the explosion:

'Brooklands

Dec 15 [1917]

Dear Miss Mary

I have received your note but have not been able to answer until now. I have been to (sic) upset with all the terror and horror of Thursday week.

I thank God it was not in the night in that would have been worse still. Oh Miss Mary the awfulness of it. I have been affected seeing many of the awful scenes of the wounded and dying lying in the streets in the snow. Everyone has done all they can to help in every way. Our house has been pretty well shattered, doors torn down, mantels broken but we have muddled through. I have got some windows boarded up for winter and a few panes put in where necessary. I was at my toilet table right by the window. I immediately dressed when I saw this awful crimson flame and black smoke rolling up in the sky. I knew in a moment what it was, I thought they had blown up our ships, before I could get to the door both windows broke into slivers and something struck me and cut me above and below my right eye I thanked God my eye was spared but I had a very narrow escape. I got downstairs and found the dining room wrecked, all glass gone, sideboard thrown across the table and everything on the floor.

Our dear neighbour soon got here. She took me to her house as she had one room not injured. Then we had to leave the house as the Dockyard was on fire close to the magazine. So we all went to a large open field where a lot of people were and stayed till danger was over. They brought out a sofa for me and everyone was so kind but it has unnerved me dreadfully. Some of my friends were badly cut. Me mine head and hand were cut, bleeding a good deal, were not serious. My eye brow and face have healed but still discoloured but I am so fearfully afraid at night. I cannot sleep, the dreadful storms day after day and cold make it worse. The suffering has been terrible. No places to take many wounded. The help from other places has been wonderful but please God not to go through this again. But enough of myself—I am so sorry poor you, left so alone. How death changes everything. Nothing is ever the same is it. I hope this will find you I could not make out the address very well. Canada was good and plain but the other Garafhax or whatever it was was not. I know how you feel about getting back to your own home. When not accustomed to company it tires one dreadfully. Dear Aunt Lill, she was so kind to me. Our house is in such confusion that it is if it is quite convenient for you please keep what dear Aunt left me for awhile until you tell me what it is, every room is in heaps, glass everywhere. We have had no meat, but once since and I feel the need of it. Now I close with very sincere sympathy for you and much love.

Yours affectionately

Cecilia

I am so thankful dear Aunt Bess is not here it certainly would have killed her.'

The remains of one family home in the Richmond District.
The fence marks a boundary that is no longer important.

Chapter 6

# THE UNITED STATES RESPONDS

*'The States weep with you Halifax*
*In this your hour of sorrow*
*They offer their help and gold*
*So don't wait till to-morrow*

*Just wade right in and help yourself*
*And we the bill will pay*
*For thats the way they do things*
*In the good old USA'*

Two verses from *Halifax in Ruins,* sung to the tune,
*The Wearing of the Green.*
Composed by an American Soldier. Sold by R.M. Martin,
Boatman, Ferry Wharf, Halifax, N.S. Price 10 cents.

New York sent prefabricated houses to provide temporary winter quarters. Chicago was too far away to send such supplies. Subscriptions of $250,000 were sent from the people of Chicago. Thomson, their mayor stated 'Halifax had been among the first to assist after the 1871 fire so Chicago should return kindness.'

The United States entered World War I three years after Canada. The Halifax explosion brought the war to the border of the United States and the destruction of an old town and many of its citizens touched them. The United States was ready to respond.

Among the first to assist were the men from the ships USS *Von Steuben* and USS *Tacoma* joining the USS *Old Colony* that was pressed into service as a hospital ship. Work parties from these and other ships headed ashore to help in rescuing and keeping people calm.

At Victoria Hall, Gottingen Street [known in 1917 as the Old Ladies Home] the blizzard came bringing snow into the Hall and the U.S.

navy boys came to batten up the windows and make the place warm for the ladies who remained. On June 6, 1918, Victoria Hall reopened accepting old and new residents. The Massachusetts Relief Fund replaced damaged furniture.

The U.S. sailors also had the grim task of searching the ruins and with others, placed the dead in the small public square at Young Street and Gottingen Street where the injured had gathered earlier.

The quickest and largest of the offers of U.S. relief came from the Commonwealth of Massachusetts.

Other states also answered the call. A collection of their responses follows:

From *The New York Times*, Friday, December 7, 1917:

'PORTLAND, Me., Dec. 6 Five car loads of supplies, including additional telegraph material, groceries, and dry goods left here tonight by special train for Halifax.

AUGUSTA, Me., Dec. 6 Governor Miliken today sent the following telegram to the Lieutenant Governor of Nova Scotia and Mayor of Halifax:

"I extend to you the deepest sympathy of the people of Maine in the terrible disaster that has stricken Halifax. Any help Maine can give is yours." '

A later telegram from the Governor of Maine:

'I am sending two thousand blankets and a thousand cots from State Military Stores (Augusta) and eight thousand other blankets from Bangor, with staff medical officers and other assistants, crews of carpenters and other voluntary workers. All ready for any emergency. Notify me of other needs.'

A newspaper article:

'December 7 Concord, New Hampshire.

Governor Henry W. Keyes this morning telegraphed the Mayor of Halifax expressing the deep sympathy of the people of New Hampshire for the stricken City and offering any possible and desired aid.'

A telegram from Cleveland Chapter, Red Cross, Cleveland, Ohio:

'Dec 8th 1917

To R.T. MacIllreith.

Chairman Relief Committee, Halifax N.S.

Have placed two thousand dollars to credit, Washington Red Cross asking them to ship from us to you most needed supplies.

Henry Shoffield.

Sect. Cleveland Chapter.'

## Selected relief donations reported in Halifax newspapers:

Citizens of Pasadena, $1,700.00, City of Tacoma, 1,580.77, Mrs. Heck and Mrs. Tener Pittsburgh, 200.00.

December 19, 1917, Department of State gave permission for US Consul General, EE Young to serve on Relief Committee Finance in Halifax.

December 22 Letter from Francis E. Willard, Settlement Bedford, Massachusetts offering house in Bedford to homeless people and to adopt children.

Some other examples: Collection by Capt. A.F. Churchill, Savannah, Georgia, $150.00; M. Jean MacNeil, Brooklyn, NY, clothing. Village of Bronxville, NY, 3 cases of clothing; messrs. Robinson & Co., Maryland, 100.00; New Hampshire citizens, Concord, NH, 8,000.00.; Fleishman Company, 1,000.00; Bishop & Company, Honolulu, second contribution, 1,128.00; V.G. Smith, Rochester, NY, fur coat; citizens of Eureka, California, 900.00; J.S. LaFontaine, Idaho, 1.00; The Lafayette Courier, Indiana, 17.25; Girls National Honor Guard, Pendleton, Oregon, 125.00; Council of Jewish Women, Terre Haute, Indiana, 100.00; Friends, Seward, Alaska, 600.00; Morning Tribune, East Liverpool, Ohio, 180.00.

There was a degree of friendly competition in fundraising as in this headline from New York newspapers:

'Dec. 19 SCHENECTADY is Helping Halifax

City of Schenectady, New York challenges other state cities to raise $4,000 to rebuild one of the destroyed houses of working men of Halifax. Slogan for Campaign "A Working man's House as a gift to Halifax."'

Dr. David Fraser Harris' *Report on the Medical Aspects of Relief in Halifax* stated: 'and a terrible catastrophe had been the occasion for that expression of practical sympathy which the quick-witted American is always ready to display.' His report continued:

'Assistance from the United States.

One of the chief features of the medical aspect of the Halifax disaster is the extreme promptness with which the great Republic to the south sent, all unsolicited, the resources of its own preparedness to the help of our stricken people. A message was received at Boston... telling in a few broken phrases of some great disaster to the old city of Halifax. That very afternoon, the Honourable Mr. McCall, Governor of the State of Massachusetts, appointed a small sub-committee of the Committee of Public Safety, the outcome of which was that a train was ordered to have steam up and be ready to start at ten p.m. that night. This it did; and, speeding on its way through a blizzard, arrived at the new South End Terminals, Halifax, on Saturday, December 8th. [As noted in Chapter 3]

Then following within an amazingly short time of the disaster came the Boston Red Cross Hospital Unit with Dr. W.E. Ladd heading 22 doctors, 69 nurses and 14 civilians plus equipment for a 560 bed hospital. And they remained until January 5, 1918 at Saint Mary's College.

Third unit was the State of Maine Hospital Unit under Major G. M. Elliott with 12 doctors, 13 nurses and 11 civilians. They took over Halifax Ladies College and stayed until December 23, 1917.

4th to arrive was the Rhode Island Chapter of American Red Cross under Major Garry deN. Hough with 52 doctors, 52 nurses and 3 civilians. While waiting for premises they made house to house visits in the devastated area.

5th group—Late evening Sunday, Dec. 9th, it was ascertained that Dr. E.A. Codman of Boston had arrived in the city with 10 doctors, 4 nurses and 9 civilians, staff of his private hospital. By Monday, the tenth, Dr. Codman's Unit was installed in the Y.M.C.A. building....

Under Dr. Codman were serving besides surgeons, nurses, and a radiologist, three obstetricians, Dr. De Normandie, Dr. Kellog and Dr. Swift.... It was therefore resolved that the Y.M.C.A. hospital should have wards set apart for obstetrical cases, a class of case which from the day of the explosion had urgently needed proper housing.

6th Group to come from the United States was a Red Cross Unit from Calais, Maine. The director of this was the Rev. R.A. Macdonald who was accompanied by 2 doctors and 9 nurses. These eager workers were distributed amongst some of the dressing stations....

On Monday, December 10th, the Medical Relief Committee received a visit from Dr. C.C. Hubly, who, with his secretary Mr. C.C. Smith, had travelled all the way from Battle Creek Sanatorium, Michigan, to the scene of the disaster. Dr. Hubly, a native of Halifax, and Mr. Smith of Chester, a town some fifty miles distant.... These gentlemen made visits from house to house, working all day, every day, until Sunday December 16th, during which time they dressed the wounds of hundreds of cases in the poorest parts of the city.'

**State of Maine Hospital Unit took over the premises of the Halifax Ladies College, Barrington Street.**

The help was appreciated. From the pages of *The New York Times*:

Sunday, December 9, 1917

'Canada's Governor General Thanks the President,

Hailing His Message of Sympathy As Sign of Unity'

OTTAWA. Dec. 8.—The Governor General [Duke of Devonshire] has sent this reply to the message of sympathy and offer of assistance from President Wilson to the City of Halifax:

"I desire to thank your Excellency for your message, which the Canadian Government and I have received with profound appreciation and gratitude.

We recognize in it and in the generous offers of assistance to the stricken City of Halifax, which have been received from many quarters of the United States a further proof of that community of feeling which unites the two peoples in a bond of mutual sympathy and interest, so particularly appropriate at the present time, when both are engaged in a common purpose to vindicate the principles of liberty and justice upon which the foundations of both Governments rest."'

Christian Lantz of Salem, Massachusetts, came to replace other volunteers. '"…and continues in a most generous and whole hearted fashion to assist and advise in the work of registration and rehabilitation." Colonel Low, Rehabilitation Committee.' In the background sun shines on floor as workman repair windows that had been boarded.

---

**Halifax newspapers ran stories of the fate of individuals:**

'Jack Ronayne 23 "a young man of splendid promise" reporter of Daily Echo telephoned his office and then went out to secure news of fire and was caught in the whirlwind of death as he approached the pier. Body found at Infirmary. (Identified by his mother)'

Archbishop Worrell, Anglican, injured in home on Lucknow Street, thrown against furniture. Windows of the Lord Bishop's church, All Saints Cathedral, Tower Road were shattered.

Lt. Colonel Armstrong injured but safe.

Isaac Creighton former Ward 6 Councillor dead.

Cora Matheson, husband at war front, safe with 2 broken legs.

Lola Burns, 8, found safe in ruins.

Captain James Murray former master of CPR Empress of Britain dead, had gone to assist at burning ship.

Captain Horatio Branman commander of Stella Maris dead, had gone to assist at collision of ships.

William McFatridge former Ward 5 councillor dead.

City Controller George Harris dead.

Alex Bond milkman dead.

Peter Burgess inspector of Nova Scotia Tramways, dead.

Conrad G. Oland brewery owner, Dartmouth, dead.

Fred Leonard Advertising representative Imperial Tobacco safe.

The Government of the United States offered one million dollars in relief aid but did not have to send it because individual Americans responded generously as can be seen from some of the telegram messages preserved at the Archives, State House, Boston and in the Relief Committee records in Halifax:

Some examples:

'MAYORS OFFICE
City of Melrose
MASSACHUSETTS
December 10th, 1917.

Hon. H. B. Endicott, Chairman,
Halifax Relief Committee,
State House, Boston, Mass.
We received your messages relative to funds for Halifax and other supplies.
We sent ten loads of clothing to the Red Cross Headquarters Saturday. On Sunday appeals were made in all the churches and at a great community service in our Memorial Building Sunday afternoon.
You may be sure that a substantial sum will be raised and sent to Robert Windsor, Treasurer. You may always depend upon cooperation in this City.'

'Chestnut Hill, Penn
Dec. 10th 1917
Chairman Relief Committee,
Halifax, N.S.

Have ready for immediate use twenty thousand surgical dressings. Glad to send you if they would be of service. Please reply my service.
Mrs E. W. Clark.'

The reply:
'Church of England Institute
Halifax, N.S.
Dec. 11th 1917
To Mrs E.W. Clark.
Chestnut Hill, Penn.
Many thanks for your kind offer. At present do not need further help but would be glad if you will keep offer open.
F. MacKelvy Bell Lieut.-Col., Chairman Medical Relief Committee'

**News of dead, injured and survivors:**
George Bowen foreman from the CGR Roundhouse and one son, James, unhurt. Mrs. Bowen is in VG Hospital with one leg amputated. Clara age 12 and Alfred age 5 have been killed.
Dec 8—18 month old found alive under stove protected by the ash pan by Pte Henneberry, Mrs. Henneberry and 5 children dead.
The Campbell brothers from Stewiacke came to help and found 3 year old boy in basement ruins alive Dec 8, 1917.
W.B. Williams—Manufacturing Jeweller, Union Street, wife and 3 children lost.
Mr. and Mrs. F.W. Killiam and family are safely at the home of Mrs. Killiam's parents, Mr. & Mrs. Henry Theakston, Seymour St. Mrs. Killiam was thought dead because clothes distributed to the needy had her letters in pockets.
Information is wanted of Alfred Carter, employed at the Hillis foundry. Mrs. Carter and family are safe at the Poor House, Truro with the exception of the baby who died on the way.
Found Unhurt—The little three year old son of Alderman and Mrs. Goodwin who was reported missing has been found and is unhurt.

## The Bottomley's 735 Robie Street:
A letter received by the author, Oct. 10, 1992.

'Dear Sir:
A friend of mine was visiting Nova Scotia. She & her husband took a tour of Halifax. She told you I was a survivor of the explosion. You asked her to have me write what I remembered. I am sending you what I remember. I don't think I will ever forget that day.

Respectfully
Mrs. Hilda Bottomley Perkins
Belmont, Vermont

The day of the Halifax explosion, I was in school at Bloomfield Street School. It was a wooden structure. They were in the process of building a new school at the time. They were putting in the foundation. Therefore I imagined when the explosion happened it was caused by the blasting for the foundation.

We were in the cloak room at the time. Everything seemed to be falling in on us. I covered my head by taking the hem of my coat and pulling the coat over my head. I cannot remember the teacher's name. The other teacher in the other room was Miss Armitage. Somehow the name North seems to come to me but I am not certain.

Our teacher was wearing a navy blue dress with a wide red belt. She called us to her. The first child took hold of her belt, each child held onto the child in front of it. She led us all safely outside. I heard later that she lost one of her eyes.

As I walked to my home at 735 Robie Street across from the cotton factory I noticed people in the street in their night clothes, and they were bleeding. People acted dazed. I remember asking someone if I was bleeding too.

When I reached home the doors and windows were blown in. The cotton factory was all in flames. My Grandmother (Mrs. Thomas Bottomley) had been injured. My father (Walker Bottomley) has just arrived home. He went up on the roof and hung rugs down the front of the house. The fire Dept. kept the rugs wet and saved the house. They realized the factory across the street couldn't be saved.

My cousin (also Walker Bottomley) was in a house on Agricola St. and it blew him the length of the house out the window. He received a head injury just above his ear.

Our house was large. A five bedroom house we had just moved into that year. The explosion lifted it and set it back on the foundation (3) three inches off square.

My grandfather (Thomas Bottomley) who operated a sash factory there was going into the boiler room to see what had happened.

He was blown in against the granite foundation. It bruised

**Hilda Bottomley attended Bloomfield School.**

**The Cotton factory ruins across from Hilda Bottomley's house on Robie Street.**

his leg. He died years later of this injury. He thought it was just a bruise. It had injured the bone.

Later in the day some man came down Robie Street and said there was to be another explosion. My grandfather took my grandmother, cousin and me to an empty lot till he was sure all was over. Then he came and took us home.

We had a cannon ball come through the roof into one of the bedrooms.

They came along the street with flat wagons and took the bodies away by wagon loads.

Our family were really lucky. My grandmother and cousin were attended by one of the American Doctors that came to help, and they recovered completely.

I hope I never see such a thing again. It's something I will never forget.

Hilda Bottomley Perkins'

Western Union Telegrams from Massachusetts towns included:

'Concord has to date raised twelve hundred fifty dollars account Halifax Relief Fund. Dalton has raised $756.73. Pittsfield $673.34. Brimfield have forty nine dollars still working mass meeting tomorrow. Money raised in Brookline now amounts to about five thousand seven hundred dollars. Holyoke Chamber of Commerce pledges $5,000. Braintree sends 1044.85, promises more. Fitchburg $14,718.64. Chicopee Falls has subscribed fifteen hundred.'

Americans were concerned about friends and family; replies were quickly sent:

'December 18, 1917.

Mrs. L.C. Lennerton, 10 Hortham Park, Dorchester, Mass.

Dear Madame:

We have received a telegram from Halifax notifying us that John, Alice, Ethel and Margaret Lennerton of Windmill Road, Dartmouth, about whom you inquired are reported as being all right.

Very truly yours,

Information Bureau Massachusetts Halifax Relief Committee'

For some, the news was sad. On December 16 Boston papers reported:

'Nearly a thousand persons attended a memorial service for victims of the Halifax explosion held yesterday in the Arlington Street Unitarian Church under the direction of the Federation of Churches of Greater Boston.

The service was arranged to afford those unable to attend funerals of friends or relatives in Halifax, a solemn and dignified substitute.

Governor McCall described the relief work in Halifax done by Massachusetts and said that the ready response to the appeal for help was one of the bright sides of the disaster.

"The men and women who died in Halifax fall in our holy cause just as truly as those who died in the trenches" declared Reverend Horr of Newton Theological School.'

The disaster was featured on the front pages of newspapers around the world. The United States which had just entered the war took a special interest as seen in the *The Pittsburgh Sun* and the *New York Times* headlines.

THE PITTSBURGH SUN — CLOSING STOCKS — FINAL

VOL. XII., NO. 238.    THE CLEAN NEWSPAPER.    PITTSBURGH, THURSDAY, DECEMBER 6, 1917.    SNOW FLURRIES TONIGHT.    TWO CENTS.

MANY PERSONS KILLED AND INJURED WHEN MUNITION-LADEN SHIP BLOWS UP AT HALIFAX; FLAMES SWEEPING CITY

An editorial cartoon from *The Evening Mail*, Halifax, captioned, "Thanks Samuel! Your heart is as big as your country is broad. You have Canada's heartiest gratitude."

Wilbert Forrest Davidson was age 9 when he started work to help support his family. He was 14 on the day of the Halifax Explosion and was working inside a large boiler at the time and survived while others around him died. He lost his sister, Margaret Henrietta age 25. Later he wrote his thoughts on the disaster regarding American relief efforts:

'And from across the border came a voice from Uncle Sam.

Saying hold on down there Halifax we're coming on the land.

There were doctors, there were Nurses, there were medical supplies, clothing, blankets and food also galore,

And their Box Cars they reached down the track probably a mile or more

The nurses they were lovely, the Doctors they were swell

And they all stayed in Halifax until the people all got well.

Now all you Nova Scotians as we go down through the years

We can walk the streets of Halifax and brush away our fears

And when you meet these good people please don't you be shy

Put your hands across the border and lift the Stars and Stripes up high.'

# MUNITION SHIP EXPLOSION
## KILLS THOUSANDS IN HALIFAX

### Great Naval Base of Britain in Nova Scotia Almost Wiped Out

Over Two Square Miles of City Turned Into a Waste of Ruin and Death by the Fiery Blast and the Fires That Followed in Its Wake—Buildings Collapse Under the Terrific Shock, Burying Their Occupants in the Ruins, and Whole Streets Are Leveled to the Ground—Thousands Injured, Thousands Homeless and Activities of the Great Seaport Paralyzed—Relief From Many Canadian Cities and From the United States Pouring Into the Stricken City—Exact Number of Dead May Never be Known.

Top: Searchers at Richmond School. Bottom: A Utica, New York newspaper story, December 8, 1917.

# Chapter 7

# THE BRITISH EMPIRE CONTRIBUTES

*'The Governor General has received this message*
*from the King:*
*Buckingham Palace, London,*
*Dec. 8, 1917*

*Most deeply regret to hear of serious explosion at Halifax, resulting*
*in great loss of life and property. Please convey to people of Halifax,*
*where I have spent so many happy times, my true sympathy in this*
*grievous calamity.*

*(Signed) George R. I.'*
As published in Canadian newspapers.

Left: Queen Mary and George V.
Right: The Governor General of Canada, the Duke of
Devonshire and his wife, the Duchess of Devonshire.

Halifax had welcomed Royal visitors since the 1780s. Male members of the Royal Family often spent time in Halifax while serving in the Royal Navy. This was reflected in the message of the King George V to his Canadian Governor General.

In 1916 Victor Cavendish, 9th Duke of Devonshire had been sworn-in at Province House in Halifax to start his 5 year term as Governor General of Canada. As the King's representative he would direct some of the relief efforts. The Duke and his wife, Evelyn, would visit Halifax December 20, and 21, 1917. The couple visited all the hospitals and shelters to express their sympathy. On December 28, 1917, a Sister of Charity of St. Patrick's Convent wrote: 'Nurses and patients at our Infirmary were cheered and helped last week by the visit of the Duke and Duchess of Devonshire.'

Local newspapers would report that the Duchess 'herself handed a flower to each of the patients, by her graciousness and sweetness brought cheer to many a suffering one.' Later a street in the Richmond District would be named in their honour.

The message of Duke of Devonshire to Nurses:
'As Governor General of Canada I am glad of having the opportunity of thanking you for your excellent service. The work you have achieved will go down thru history…you have willingly and nobly borne your share of the burden and I am more than pleased with the way the work was organized and managed.'

*The Times* [London] kept the people of Great Britain informed as the following stories note:

'MAKING GOOD THE LOSS A TASK OF ALL

Ottawa, Dec. 10—Trainloads of supplies and many doctors and nurses have arrived from the United States.—Reuter.

Halifax, Dec. 10—Sir Robert Borden, who is member for Halifax, has cancelled his political engagements to devote his time to relief work.—Exchange Telegraph Company.'

'THE TIMES, TUESDAY, DECEMBER 11, 1917

MANSION HOUSE RELIEF FUND.

CONTRIBUTIONS BY THE ROYAL FAMILY.

Chas A. Hanson Lord Mayor of London…

"To any Lord Mayor of London it would have been an urgent duty to take the lead in a matter of this kind but me personally having spent many years in Canada the privilege is especially welcome."

The Lord Mayor has received the following letter, dated December 10, from Sir Frederick Ponsonby, Keeper of his Majesty's Privy Purse:

"I have it in command from the King to forward the enclosed cheque for £1,000 as a subscription from his Majesty towards the Fund which you are raising for the relief of the sufferers in the Halifax disaster.

The King feels sure that your appeal will be generously responded to by the public, who will welcome this opportunity of showing their profound sympathy at this terrible tragedy which has befallen the people of Canada."

The Lord Mayor also received: From Queen Mary £300; Queen Alexandra, £200; Edward the Prince of Wales, £300; the Duke of Connaught, £500.

Messrs. Furness, Withy, and Co. (Limited) have sent £5,000 to the Lord Mayor, who has himself contributed £105 and the Lady Mayoress £52 10s.

The Lord Mayor has received from the High Commissioner for Canada (Sir George Perley) the following cable which has reached him from Sir Robert Borden:

"The disaster is appalling in its magnitude and its results. Between one and two square miles of the city completely wiped out, and 15,000 to 20,000 people rendered homeless and many of them destitute. A conservative estimate of the killed is 1,500, and many thousands injured. I have spent the afternoon in hospitals and the cases are most distressing.…"'

In Halifax newspapers it was reported that the war was costing Britain $33 million daily. The headline for Thursday, December 13, 1917, a week after the explosion read:

'NOTWITHSTANDING ITS STRESS AND TREMENDOUS FINANCIAL BURDEN, THE DEAR MOTHER LAND GIVES $5,000,000 TO HELP REBUILD HALIFAX.'

The money was granted during a speech by Mr. Andrew Bonar Law, the Chancellor of the Exchequer. He makes mention of his mother, Eliza Kidston, from the Kidston family in Spryfield, Nova Scotia. The Chancellor would become Prime Minister of Great Britain.

House of Commons, London, England, remarks of Mr. Bonar Law, the Chancellor of Exchequer:

'There is only one other subject on which I think it right to say a word before I sit down. The house, I am sure, has read with the deepest sympathy the account of the terrible disaster at Halifax, Nova Scotia. (Hear, hear.) It is a disaster which in peace time would have filled all our minds, and even now, when the devastation of the war occupies us so much, there is ground for special sympathy with the people of that city. As it happens it is a city with which I have myself very intimate relations. My mother was born there. It is one of the best-known cities in the Dominion of Canada; the harbour in which the disaster took place is one of the best and one of the most beautiful in the world. The disaster is really appalling. From the city of Halifax at

the beginning of the war men came most readily and most enthusias-
tically to play their part in the war (cheers), and I know also that very
many have fallen…to-day it is our intention that the Prime Minister
should send in the name of the Cabinet as a whole a message of sympathy coupled with a donation, which will be paid for, I presume, out
of this Vote of Credit, of a million sterling. (Loud cheers.) I have mentioned this with this object in view, that when we send a message it will
go to the people of Halifax and to the people of the Dominion with the
certain knowledge that the sympathy expressed is not that of the
Government alone, but that it is shared, and shared in equal strength;
by the members of the British House of Commons. (Cheers.).'

Thanks from Canada was duly reported in *The Times*:

'THE HALIFAX DISASTER. CANADA'S REPLY TO THE WAR CABINET

The Duke of Devonshire, Governor General of Canada has sent the
following reply, dated December 13, to the message of the War Cabinet:

My Ministers on behalf of people of Halifax and of all Canada
desire me to express their profound appreciation of your message. This
magnificent expression of sympathy from people of United Kingdom
will be received by all Canadian people as an abundant evidence of
that unity of purpose and effort which animates entire Empire. Your
message has been communicated to Mayor of Halifax and Mayor of
Dartmouth and it will do much to comfort and sustain many thousands who have been bereaved.'

While Halifax struggled to make its citizens comfortable, all sections
of the British Empire were responding to the needs of the survivors.
The dominion governments sent large sums. Individuals from those
countries would also contribute: Australia's donations would total
$250,000, New Zealand, $50,000. Jamaica immediately sent 1,000
pounds to His Excellency the Lt.-Governor of Nova Scotia from the
Governor and Council. Government of Trinidad and Tobago sent

A boarded-up storefront used for the posting of notices.

Saint Joseph's Hall, Gottingen Street was bent by force of
the explosion. The hall was repaired and used as supply
depot.

$4,800. On January 2, 1918, it was reported that the Colony of Hong Kong sent $50,000 for the relief of the Halifax sufferers.

Closest to Halifax was Newfoundland. [not joining Canada until 1949] A few days after the explosion the Executive Council voted $50,000 for Halifax. This was a large amount for a colony that would almost bankrupt itself sending men and material to the war. Supplies and money would be added to this initial amount. Agents for Newfoundland came to Halifax to look after the many citizens resident in the city. Some accepted transport home. Others sent word back that they had survived. Two children of the School for the Deaf would go home safely but on the return voyage from Newfoundland to restart school they would drown with others in a shipwreck.

George Emmett (right), the owner of row of buildings finds 150 shillings in the ruins of his two stores. In the background (top left) is Wellington barracks.

So much in supplies arrived in Halifax that the committees had to ask people to stop sending until it was determined what was needed. Money for reconstruction was always welcome and continued to come in well into 1919. The exact value of goods will never be known and researchers will never determine what money was given as it was sent to so many different groups and committees. Foreign countries and their citizens would respond as can be seen from lists. Some countries, states and provinces gave on behalf of their people. A review of donor columns in local newspapers shows a diverse group of people sending money. Donor names are not always available as companies and newspapers established subscriptions that were then wired in lump payments to Halifax. These are some examples:

Kingston, Jamaica, 200. U.S. Ship in Port, 222. City of Detroit, 5,000. Edward Kennedy, New York, 50. Miss Bessie Thrall, Chicago, 2. A friend, Hamilton, Bermuda, 125. Miss Louise Thrall, Chicago, 1. Basseterre, St. Kitts, 2,400. Chamber of Commerce, New York, 5,000. Arthur Brady, Santa Elena, Ecuador, 25. City of St. John's, Newfoundland, 10,000. Boston Insurance Co., 50,000. City of Miami, Florida, 250. Chamber of Commerce, Kansas City, 5,000.

Telegrams of sympathy were received from the British Empire and foreign nations including:

Bermuda… 'our profound regret at the great misfortune which has fallen upon the city to which Bermuda is united by many bonds.'

President Poincare of France to King George V:

'I wish to express to Your Majesty on the occasion of the sad catastrophe at Halifax my deepest sympathy and I beg of you kindly to forward to the people of Canada the cordial and fateful remembrance of the French people.'

'…convey to the Government of Canada in the name of the Government of Switzerland the expression of deep felt sympathy.'

Dec. 7 'All Italy and all Italians are grieved at the terrible disaster which has stricken Halifax. Will you accept our deepest sympathy.' Zunini, Consul General

The German Government press *Kolnische-Zeitung* would state 'Not without emotion can one hear the news of the devastation of the hard hit Canadian City.' As the munitions were meant for use against their soldiers, no donation would be forthcoming.

Among the offers of help for Halifax was a letter sent to Ottawa from the prisoners of war at Amherst, Nova Scotia. The Relief Committee was unsure of what to do with this offer as it had not yet been established if the explosion had been an enemy plot. In the first week of January 1918 in the newspaper column titled 'Halifax Relief Fund Acknowledgments,' the donation was listed between the Vancouver Medical Association Vancouver BC $10 and the Pennsylvania railway Women's Division for War relief Washington DC $114, 'collected among Prisoners of War at Amherst $66.55.'

Showing no distinction between large and small donors and following together in the same fund column, *Halifax Herald*, December 1917:
  'Government Dominion of Canada $1,000,000
  Mrs. Marjorie Solon, Tenafly, New Jersey $5'
Other examples of donations:
  Employees, Dept. Of State, War Relief Work, Wash, DC, $ 300.00
  American troops on board transport, 2,110.08
  Miss Catherine Clarkson, New York, N.Y., 1,000.00
  "A Scotch Woman," Pittsburgh, Pa., 10.00
  Children of Saint Margaret College, Versailles, Ky., 10.00
  Mike Thomas, Hollandale, Wisconsin, 10.00
  Sir Charles Gordon, British War mission to U.S., 1,000.00
  Baptist Hospital nurses and patients, Brookline, Mass., 203.00
  Readers of Omaha Daily News, 500.00

Government of Bermuda installment, 3,840.00
Chamber of Commerce, Port of Spain, Trinidad, 3,000.00
Chicago Committee, 25,000.00
Boys Zion Church, Louisville, Kentucky, 11.00
Lord Mayor of Liverpool, England, $23,861.11
Bishop and Co., Honolulu, 1,000.00
Santa Barbara, Calif., 500.00
Immanuel Danish Lutheran Church Ladies Aid, Racine Wis., 10.00
A patriotic Maury County Farmer, Columbus, Tennessee, 25.00
Trinidad, British West Indies, 500.00
Town of Enfield, Conn., 195.26
Scoville Mfg. Co., Waterville, Conn., 5,000.00
Halifax Relief Fund, Walla Walla, Wash., 275.80
City of Hartford, Conn., 5,000.00
Two Canadians, Redlands, 2.00
Mayor of St. John's, Nfld., 3rd subscription, 10,000.00
Presser Foundation, Philadelphia, 1,000.00
Syracuse War Chest, N.Y., 10,000.00
C.R. Wright, Frankton, Indiana, 5.00
A Texas Barber, Collection, Dallas, 5.00
Jolley Hardwood Col, Milton, Iowa, 10.00
James Laughlan, Boise, Idaho, 200.00
Aquillino Fuente, Havana, Cuba, 15.00
British Red Cross and Order St. John, 125,000.00
Dec. 22 To Date, $2,112,028.66

News and fundraising appeared on the same pages of Halifax newspapers:
  'Dec. 19 Mr. Boutillier dies St. Mary's Hospital, left wife and 2 children.
  Newark Evening News Fund, Newark, N.J., $ 1,000.00
  Harvey War Relief League, Harvey, Ill., 100.00

Collected by Bowring and Co., New York, 12,000.00

City of Chicago, first payment, 50,000.00

Miss Mary Armitage, Bloomfield School severely cut—this dedicated teacher looked after safety of her children. Miss Clark, Alexandra School—it is feared will lose her sight.'

News briefs were mixed with donation notices:

'Sir Robert Borden in Halifax With American Relief Workers'

'Collision Enquiry Shows Confusion Existed Regarding Signals'

Mrs. J. A. Caribett, Medicine Hat—2 boxes children's clothing

D.C. Chisholm, Toronto—one 7 passenger Automobile

Marjorie Johnston Mowat, Miami, Florida—4 boxes of supplies

Thompson Red Cross, Thompson, Conn.—3 barrels of clothing

Samuel Park, Principal, Easton, Pa.—2 boxes clothing

New York relief committee—one car load canned goods

Shoe Firms of Boston give 5000 pairs of hard to come by rubber footwear.

'$450 From Baltimore Doctor W. W. Russell who has a summer residence in Chester, "to help relieve the distress in Halifax."'

While citizens tried to cope with their losses they sought to maintain some of the customs and standards of the era.

On Dec. 8, 1917, Chicago's *Daily News* carried this editorial cartoon to illustrate that 'war's devastation' in Europe had reached to Halifax claiming 'another victim.'

## The Hurleys of 43 Allan Street:

The author became friends with the Hurley sisters as a child and knew them by their nicknames 'Girlie' and 'Hurley.'

Helen 'Hurley' Hurley lived on Allan Street with her sister Cecilia 'Girlie' and their parents. The girls were attending Oxford Street School. The school was Catholic and in 1917 seven Sisters of Charity from Saint Joseph's Convent were teaching there. On December 6 the windows were shattered but being some distance from the harbour there were few serious injuries.

Helen was 7 and remembered 'we were on our knees saying morning prayers and there was a small explosion then a big one and the glass blew in. Sister rang the bell on her desk and told us to go downstairs and outside. For some reason the boys carried us on their backs. I was on Clyde Gray's back and Margaret Horne was on the boy behind me. There was quite a crush of people in the hall. I had a cut just above my eyes and was lucky not to have lost my sight. We were all allowed to run home. My sister, Girlie, was sent to check the relatives at Hurley Lane. [now Young St. at Oxford.] When she tried to return the soldiers would not let her back into the neighbourhood. Meanwhile Mother and I went with others to Rosebank [a subdivision of large homes that was just being built] to wait for permission to return home. I remember my father was working and he said the wagon he was driving to the job jumped up when the explosion happened. It was awhile before we got back to school and things were not nice for a time.'

Cecilia was 10 and as the older of the girls she was sent to see how others in the family were. She had many thoughts running through her mind as she passed fields and small estates to the farmhouse on Hurley Lane. Not being allowed to return home she was sent from the farmhouse over to Hurley Crest a small private convalescent sanitorium run by her Aunt, the Widow Margaret Hurley. Hurley Crest was soon busy with the treating of the wounded including Sisters of Charity of Saint Joseph's School and Convent which was destroyed by the blast. The brave little girl helped as best she could. Cecilia was later reunited with her sister and parents. Their father Reuben was in the building trade so their house was soon closed in. At that time they were still using oil lamps so they were well supplied with light. Hurley Crest was used as a dressing station in the weeks after the disaster.

'Girlie' married and served as secretary to Roman Catholic Archbishops of Halifax. 'Hurley' never married and lived with her sister. Hurley Crest was donated to the church and the site is now location for Saint Catherine of Siena Rectory, Bayers Road.

Oxford Street School was used as Infectious Diseases Hospital.

Mrs. Maude Foley,
Streetcar Conductor,
1917-1918

A election notice intended to persuade women to vote for
the government party. Women were only entitled to vote if
they had a male relative who served in the war.

'The Halifax Tram Company is to be com-
mended for Employing Women Conductors;
Why Not Women Drivers Also.' 'of course it
will be said that women can't get to work
early in the morning or work as late as 11 or
12 at night and especially that they can't
stand the exposure to the Halifax climate.
But what the English and French and Italian
and American women can do Halifax
women can do equally as well and with
equal cheerfulness and determination.'
—The *Halifax Herald*, December 22, 1917.

## Chapter 8

# SOCIAL STANDARDS OF THE ERA

*'Proprietor of a flourishing grocery business in the Northend and an ex chairman of the Board of School Commission, to whose interest Richmond school owes a large debt. He is a progressive and public spirited man and always in the fore in movements related to the advancement of Northend interests. He is in religious faith a Presbyterian and is most active and helping in the Grove Church of which he is a member. He is thoroughly identified with the life of the district in which he lives and one of its representative man.'*

A Tribute to Constant Upham that appeared
in the *Halifax Herald*, November 5, 1917.

The stories in the local newspapers during 'The War to End All Wars' would be a mixture of sad news, patriotic promotions, cheery home notes and stories reflecting changing times and the standards of the era.

In the *Halifax Herald* ran a series: 'Well known Halifax Men.' On Monday, Nov. 5 the profile was of Ex Alderman Constant Upham.

One month later the notice would read 'Upham Mr. & Mrs. and 2 children DEAD.'

Further reports in the newspapers would state that 'Constant Upham was the store keeper who telephoned in the fire on the Mont Blanc to the fire department. His brother Martin Upham left the store to do deliveries and was saved from the destruction that killed the former Alderman, "the young lady employees" and most of the firemen.

Martin Upham saw his own house collapse killing his wife but he was able to save two children.'

Despite the hardships caused by the explosion, social standards had to be maintained. This fact is illustrated in the written material regarding the disaster.

In the report of Mr. Ratchesky to the Governor of Massachusetts:

'On the day of our arrival (Dec. 8, 1917) we were entertained by Premier Sir Robert Borden at the Halifax Club, where the Premier made arrangements for the housing of the doctors of the unit, the Red Cross people, the newspaper men and myself. The club ordinarily has no sleeping facilities, and I am told that it is the first time in its history that beds have been set up. The nurses were quartered at private homes near the hospital, four of them being entertained at Government House, which is the Governor's private residence.'

In the report of Major Giddings of Massachusetts:

'A pleasing incident occurring this same day (Dec. 10) was a request from Colonel Bell that the commanding officer personally visit at Government House, the official residence of the Lieutenant-Governor, the son of Admiral Charles E. Kingsmill, who had been injured at the time of the explosion. The lad was more or less cut about the face, but fortunately was not seriously injured, and was taken to Ottawa the next afternoon by his father.'

After repairs to the premises of Halifax newspapers, stories were published that would not report names or just use initials to protect the privacy of those written about. Reports used wording that now seems inappropriate. The headline of Dec. 18 regarding the former Devil's Island lighthouse keeper and his wife reads like a script from a silent movie of the time:

'After more than twenty-five years of Faithful Service, George Faulkner and Wife, who came to the City to live in Quietude a week before the disaster, were hurled into Eternity with Dramatic Suddenness.'

Other news stories also echo the language of the era:

'The Thrilling Story of the Heart Breaking Experience of Captain Sitland in His Futile Search for His Five Missing Children' 'His eldest son Willie 14 yrs attending Bloomfield School safe. Wife seriously injured at Cogswell Street Hospital.'

'Sir Frederick Fraser and Lady Fraser have offered their little son's nursery to all the children who as a result of the great catastrophe have lost their sight. Master Fred is very keen indeed to have the small sufferers come in, very eager to do his bit to make them happy.'

'Mr. Fisher, an oil merchant well known throughout the city, whose home was at 105 1/2 Gottingen Street had his house completely destroyed, his wife being badly cut and having one arm broken while he has lost the sight of one eye.'

'A sad case which has come to the attention of the Investigation Committee was that of Mrs. "J" whose family of seven were rendered homeless by the explosion and sought refuge at the home of a daughter at South Clifton Street. Here eleven persons were found living in one room the house having been sadly wrecked.'

'Boston Unit entertained at home of Hon. F.B. McCurdy,' may now sound out of place, but people did have to eat and relax from awful sights of disaster.

Stanley K. Smith, Editor of the *Daily Telegraph*, Saint John, New Brunswick came to Halifax to report the story of the explosion and later wrote a book in 1918, *Heart Throbs of the Halifax Horror*. He had a long train ride to Halifax and was very hungry. First he accepted some chocolate nut bars at a little store. Then he entered the only door of the Queen Hotel, Hollis St. not boarded up. Despite the destruction around him he was able to write in poetic terms of his dinner:

'One of the wonders of the disaster is the fact that the Queen Hotel and its neighbour the Halifax kept their cuisine unimpaired... soup was the introduction, salmon provided a little flirtation, asparagus on toast was the entree, roast chicken and port meant getting well acquainted, plum pudding gave an opportunity for spooning, bread and cheese was the plain married life after the delectable stuff and the finger bowls were there for the christening.

Paper napkins made their appearance the next day but this was the only departure from the routine.'

Overwhelmed by what he saw outside the hotel, he quickly departed for home by train. On the trip to New Brunswick he would note 'passing splendid steel cars of American Relief Trains on their errand of mercy.'

The disaster was also used to make social comment. Dr. Willis Bryant Moore MD from Kentville wrote concerning women and the right to vote:

'I am sure the most hardened opponent of the extension of the franchise to women would have been a convert had he witnessed, as I did, their qualities of initiative, brains, and efficiency, under such circumstances as would test to the fullest degree such qualities in man.'

On the front page of the *Halifax Herald*, side by side with the reports of the terrible destruction in Halifax, ran a story about the Duke of Portland's daughter and ladies of the upper classes being greeted by the King in an ammunition factory in England. It was considered a shining example of how everyone should be doing their bit for the war effort. One can almost hear the trumpets sounding the call to arms.

Some stories were reported for their lighter side:

A lady was chased down the street by a man with a coat. She did not realize the explosion had blown off her clothes and he was only offering her covering.

A mother staying at the Halifax Hotel [on Hollis Street] while seeing off her son, a gunner, for overseas insisted after the blast that staff still bring her the tea so she could finish her breakfast. She felt her son would need his tea for the day ahead. [In later years, Mrs. Puddicombe

On the morning of December 6, women were preparing food for the day. Some might have been reading a *Calendar of Dinners with 615 Recipes* including the story of CRISCO, Price 25 cents. For that evening it was suggested the meal consist of: 'Caviar Canapes, Roast Duck, Apple Sauce, Canned Beans, Mashed Potatoes, Tomato Jelly Salad, Apple Dumplings, Raisins, Nuts, Coffee.' Of course the sponsor provided the apple sauce recipe which included using Crisco.

The disaster caused the loss of foodstuffs and Christmas supplies so that by the evening of the disaster many survivors went hungry. Edith Murphy [Hartnett] remembers when supplies did arrive they were often only one item, the abundance of maple cookies put her off them for 80 years.

would see her son become a Supreme Court Judge.]

In the Fraser Harris Report: 'Nothing, however tragic, is wholly without its amusing incidents. One girl, when the explosion occurred, had evidently been interrupted in her dressing. Save for her corsets, she might be said to have been "wrapped in thought", but thus attired she started, valise in hand, and found herself on the Common, then thronged with a vast concourse of people. All of a sudden she seemed to realize her condition. Without a word, she sat down suddenly on the grass, opened the bag, and, taking from it all it contained, began with feverish haste to complete her dressing. She had brought away nothing with her except a pair of green silk stockings and a pair of white satin shoes. But, attired in these, delicate and precious garments, she continued her flight.'

Third Officer Mayers of the SS *Middleton Castle* was quoted in December 1917, *Halifax Herald* that 'he was sent flying from the deck of his ship to Fort Needham 1/2 mile through the air with only minor injuries, all he had on was one boot. And considered himself lucky.' [He later became a river pilot in Liverpool England.] Others who were lucky were those who awoke on the wagons or in the rooms for the dead. Those who discovered them certainly had a story to tell.

---

Dec. 29, 1917 *The Canadian Courier* published a drawing by Arthur Lismer, principal of Victoria School of Art & Design, Halifax to accompany the story 'When War Came to Halifax.' The caption of the drawing of fleeing crowds reads: 'Fearing a second Explosion old and young Refugees, suddenly left homes and all they had, to flee—they scarcely knew whither or what from.'

---

One of the best examples of restrained behaviour of the time was that of the Principal of the Victoria School of Art and Design, Arthur Lismer.

Lismer age 31, would write that he had missed his train from Bedford so was not injured like others on way to work. He, his wife and daughter escaped flying glass that smashed through their home. As an Artist he might have been on the war front like many of his contemporaries but had no interest in that. Yet he ended up seeing scenes that many military men would describe as worse than what they saw in France. He sketched drawings of the scenes in Halifax for publication. Of immediate concern were his family and students. The condition of his school and works on loan for his gallery were also concerns. 'My school is now filled with coffins.' He quickly contacted the National Gallery of Canada to tell them of the fate of lithographs, frames and glass. His gentlemanly letter starts with his sadness for the people of Halifax, next he almost apologizes for what has happened to the art works. He intended to reopen his school just after Christmas so he asks the Director of the National Gallery if he might keep 14 pieces of unbroken picture glass for use in the windows. The Director, Mr. Brown, was quite quick to reply that the glass could be kept.

The school would reopen, but it would be some time before a show would be displayed in the gallery.

There is also correspondence as Arthur Lismer tried to persuade the President of Dalhousie University to replace destroyed art work with that by local artists but to no avail. President MacKenzie thought patrons of the University would like to see copies of their original gifts that were copies of famous art so in the end Principal Lismer provided catalogues of pictures and sculptures from London.

Arthur Lismer would later leave Halifax and become one the Canadian Group of Seven—artists known for their landscapes.

No matter what level of society the response to the disaster was overwhelming for Halifax. All amounts given were truly appreciated as the

A view looking south along Argyle Street. The corner building is the Victoria School of Art and Design. The school principal, Arthur Lismer wrote, 'my school is now filled with coffins.' Next door, Snow's Funeral Undertakers, had limited space, so bodies were embalmed, placed in coffins and burial boxes. These were then placed outside along the sidewalks stretching north towards city hall. Families would then arrange for services in their homes or in the few churches safe for use.

following release by the Relief Committee shows. It appeared in local newspapers January 4, 1918, and again reflects the language of the era:

'One of the most outstanding cases of sympathy and generosity that has yet to come to the attention of the Relief Committee is that of Carl White, a porter in the employ of the Pullman company who pulled into Halifax last night in charge of a car on a special train from New York. This morning, this dusky gentleman with a pleasant smile and pearly white teeth walked into the secretary's office and handed in a dollar for the Relief Fund. But the expression of sympathy that accompanied it made it look as big as some of the five hundred and thousand dollar cheques that had arrived in the morning mail.'

## Home of the Guardian Angel, Brunswick Street:

As told to S. Maureen Regan by Sister Mary Eucharia and published in *Changing Times*, May 1994

On December 6, 1917, the Halifax Explosion occurred. The fire escape door was ripped off its hinges, and a baby was killed when a heavy water tank fell and crushed it. All the other babies were unhurt, not even scratched, although their cribs were covered with glass and splinters.

Fearing a second explosion, authorities advised the sisters to take the babies to the Commons. On the long walk to the Commons each sister carried a baby. Soldiers in trucks transported some of the children.

Sister Eucharia recounted the amusing story of a soldier with bright red hair holding baby Hughie, also with bright red hair, accompanied by Sister Clemens whose lovely red hair showed under her black bonnet. It was a study in reds!

After the explosion, a baby was found alive in an ash can. The parents and family had all been killed. The baby, Richard Shea, came to the Home, and later, through many years, stayed in touch with the sisters who had brought him up. [15 members of the Shea family killed] The sisters returned to the Home to find heat and water supplies cut off. A kind neighbour, Mrs. Buchanan, heated water and brought it into the Home as it was needed. Father MacKinnon in Herring Cove offered the use of his Glebe, but it was thought wiser to stay in the city. After midnight Mass at Christmas, the roof began to leak and babies had to be brought downstairs. After a time, the Home was repaired and painted. One outstanding improvement was the replacing of straw ticks with real mattresses on all the cribs and beds.

[Sister Mary Eucharia died in 1999, age 104.]

Home of the Guardian Angel, the former Merkel Mansion where staff and 72 babies occupied the large ballroom because of leaks in the roof.

This motor car, with tires removed, had been suspended in a garage on Agricola Street for the winter.

'"Commandeering" was a word much in vogue that day. Perhaps the most urgent need was for transportation. With many sufferers, rapid transit to the hospital or dressing station, was a matter of life and death. A rumour flew about that all vehicles had been commandeered by military orders. Colonel Thompson's general orders were, "Wherever you want a car or a team, stop and take it." Cars were appropriated under the owner's nose and many a car was worn out that day by unskillful and too zealous drivers.'—From the report of the Halifax Disaster, by Archibald MacMechan.

'Halifax is a city built on the side of a steep hill. During winter it has not been the custom to use motor cars to any great extent, and with the blizzards that followed one on top of the other in swift succession what cars were obtainable were one after the other frozen up and left in gutters here and there in different parts of the city.'—From a letter of the Relief Commission to the *Yale News*.

For some institutions like the cloistered Convent of Sacred Heart boarding school for girls, on Spring Garden Road, the disaster presented unusual circumstances. The notice announcing the establishment of the Convent as an emergency dressing station advised: 'for all to conduct themselves accordingly!' The girls were sent home or to a convent in Montreal.

Duplex at Duffus and Agricola Streets that would be repaired.

A view of the corner of Gottingen and Kaye Streets with soldiers guarding houses. The north wall of Saint Joseph's Convent can be seen on right.

Chapter 9

# RETURN TO DAILY LIFE

*'For homeless Rent 4 rooms and bath $12,*
*2 rooms no bath $5'*
*'50 cents to attend a matinee'*
*'Lumber at $28 per thousand feet'*
*'Burials $30 per adult body, $20 youth, $15 child.'*

From the records of the Relief Commission
and Halifax newspapers, 1917-18.

The west side of St. Joseph's School facing Gottingen
Street.

Not all stories of survival would reach the newspapers. In later years people would recall their stories of injuries and separation. It took months and sometimes years for people to regain a normal daily life.

## Philip Smith Family, 25 Kaye Street:

'Mamma, Phil and Anna were at home. Papa was at work in Woodside. William had just begun his first year at Holy Heart Seminary. Gerald was attending Saint Mary's College High School and Margaret and Gertrude[author] were students at St. Joseph's School.

At 9:00 a.m. a terrific roar and piercing light, both impossible to describe, ushered in the horrible devastation. Suddenly, all was darkness as the floor on my second storey eighth grade classroom gave way and we were buried amidst plaster and debris below the first floor level. Then self-preservation took over. After much shoving and pushing I finally saw a ray of light, and eventually arrived at what had been the front entrance. I have no recollection of having seen any of my companions. As I looked around I saw Will coming down the street. He took me by the hand, and said, "Have you seen Margaret?" Just then she appeared from the other side of the building. With the warning not to step on any wire, we walked towards home. A man covered with blood was holding up a girl. Will said that they were Phil and Anna. He brought Anna over to a lamp post lying on the ground and asked Margaret and me to hold her up. She was, I believe, unconscious. Then he tried to help Phil rescue Mamma who was under the piano. From loss of blood Phil had lost his strength. Will came out to the front door and by pointing to his Roman collar attracted the attention of two young soldiers. They held up the piano while Will lifted Mamma from under it. There was a horse and cart coming up the hill. Will asked the driver to stop, but it was only when Will held back the horse that he consented. Will put Mamma, Anna and Phil on it. We all went to a low place, the Bog, now the area where the Hydrostone homes are built. The available ambulances, carts, and wagons in the city conveyed the sick to various hospitals and the younger people were taken by various vehicles to wherever there was accommodation. Before we left, fires were destroying what was left of the homes.

At St. Mary's College High School Gerald was hit on the head by a window frame. By the time he was able to move, we had all disappeared and he and Papa arrived about the same time in front of our house which had already been burnt. The only thing remaining out on the street was the family Bible. They went to Holy Heart Seminary where they stayed overnight.

The next day [Friday] they began to visit all the morgues in search of Anna. However, she had been taken to Camp Hill Hospital and was found the next day by Sister Mary Berchmans Haverty, one of Anna's teachers at the Mount Academy. She was very fond of Anna. Anna had lost her right eye and had many gashes in many places around her face. Really only her left eye was showing amid the bandages. Sister passed this girl lying on a mattress on the floor and said "This is Anna Smith's eye" She took Anna's hand and said, "If you are Anna Smith press my hand!'" Sister got in contact with Father Will. Anna had serious internal injuries. She was taken to the operating room several times, but to no avail. The Sisters at the Mount prayed and she was cured.

Mamma was taken to Cogswell Street Army Hospital where she was found on Sunday. Phil was sent to a hospital in Antigonish. Before we left the Bog, I saw him lying on the ground quivering from head to foot from the severing of nerves and the loss of blood.

Margaret and I were taken by the driver of our vehicle, a bread wagon I think, to the Salvation Army Hospital. That night a very heavy snowstorm occurred, and for hours on end the noise of boards being nailed to window frames resounded. All over the city glass was destroyed. On Sunday Will and another seminarian, a Mr. Thorne from Newfoundland, found us, gave us a Rosary, and assured us that they would find a boarding house for us as soon as possible.

The next day we moved into the home of a Scottish lady where on Wednesday Mamma joined us. She came by ambulance. On Thursday, one week after the explosion, Uncle Gus and Will Kennedy arrived in Halifax and took Gerald and me to Shediac to Grandma's. As Mamma was not able to be moved, it was decided that Margaret should stay with her. Margaret had a deep cut on her cheek which needed a doctor's attention. I had small cuts on my nose and head, but nothing serious.

One day a letter arrived for Gerald directing him to return to St. Mary's Academy as a boarder.…I was left alone with Grandma until February [1918] when Phil arrived with Mamma and Margaret. Then Phil returned to his work as a mail clerk on the train in Halifax. At the end of June, Anna and Father Will arrived. In late August Anna, Gerald and I began housekeeping in Halifax in a furnished house owned by one of Anna's friends, a Miss Wakely. In mid-September [1918] Mamma and Margaret joined us. The family was once again united.'

**Sister Anna Gertrude Smith SC, former professor at Mount Saint Vincent University, recorded her memories for family.**

**Newspapers and records of the Relief Committee shed light on the daily life in Dec. 1917 and early 1918:**

Coal supplies were still short so authorities wanted to buy coal from demolished businesses; Halifax would need 8,000 tons yet only 40 tons arrived in city due to snow blocking trains.

Dec. 13—search for survivors and bodies still not complete after 7 days.

Dec 14—searching harbour debris for bodies was done by the Royal Canadian Navy.

Dr. Darlington, Medical Health Department of New York offered to pay own way to Halifax to advise on sanitary services to prevent disease. Relief Committee asked he come as soon as possible.

Dec. 15—Notice in papers St. Patrick's Church—Services in Casino Theatre: 'Monsignor Murphy of St. Patrick's Church announces to his parishioners that the manager of the Casino has kindly offered the use of his theatre for services Sunday morning. Mass will be at 8, 10, 11 o'clock.'

Dec 18—*Halifax Herald* Notice—'ROTARIANS Please attend an important meeting of the Rotary Club at the new Green Lantern on Tuesday Dec. 18 at 5:30 pm. Supper will be served. Out of town Rotarians will please attend. BH Morrison, Secretary'

It was due to community groups and business response that Halifax was able to look after so many of the citizens who had no place to go. A list of locations gives a picture of how the burden was shared:

Imperial Oil in Eastern Passage donated $10,000 and asked it be directed principally for relief in Dartmouth. The company was building a new refinery in Woodside and let construction sheds be used to shelter 200 homeless.

Monastery of Good Shepherd, Mother Superior took in 77 people, some were given comfort in their final hours. Saint Michael's Laundry would do laundry of Northend residents free, just as commercial laundries had offered.

From Dr. Fraser Harris' Report:

'On the day of the explosion, the Monastery of the Good Shepherd on Quinpool Road opened their doors and admitted a large number of refugees, among them some who were badly injured by glass, etc. Although the sisters had a large number of their own inmates to look after, in a building that was badly damaged, they still made room to take in more. I want to bear testimony to the splendid work done at this institution, especially by Sisters. St. Thomas and St. Celestine, the latter of whom continued to work till she was taken ill with pneumonia, and had to be under my care for some time.'

---

**Offers of donations came by telegram, sometimes to church leaders:**

*Halifax Herald*—'Telegrams Received by Archbishop McCarthy: "Expressions of Sympathy from all over Dominion and from the United States Cardinals Forley and Begin Among Number"
San Francisco, Calif. Dec 7—"Heartfelt sympathy … Both places at Chester at your disposal. Am sending some help. Wire at my expense if friends are safe." Bishop Shahan, Pres. University of Washington
Portland Me Dec 7—"Portland Diocese will help in any way you desire. My deep sympathy." D.S. Walsh, Bishop of Portland
Toronto Dec 12—"Wired through Royal Bank two thousand for relief of St. Joseph's Parish from Toronto Parishes." N. McNeil, Archbishop of Toronto
Boston Dec 11— "Would clothing for fifty small boys and girls be acceptable and useful. Telegraph answer and instructions. Home for Destitute Catholic Children."'

From the Fraser Harris Report:

'The Emergency Hospital at the Waegwoltic Club House—Not long before the end of the year December 24th, the club house known as the Waegwoltic, situated in beautiful grounds near the head of the North West Arm, was prepared as a temporary hospital.

At no one time were there more than forty patients in the hospital. During January and February, certain of the fourth year medical students of Dalhousie acted as interns here. The hospital was closed on February 28th.'

In the suburb of Rockingham summer cottages as well as mansions were opened for the people. The Sherwood and the Wayside Inn were full to the attic with those in need. Seeking shelter in these or public buildings or with friends, many homeless were able to avoid staying in the 400 tents put up on the Commons by the Engineers and Ordinance Corps. A number who did stay in the tents froze to death.

There were survivors too proud, too injured, had no clothes to go out or felt others were worse off so they did not seek assistance. Miss Jessie Forbes of New York led a committee of 100 to list needs of people in house to house canvass in Dartmouth. Others took on similar work in Halifax.

Voluntary Aid Divisions [VAD's] helped wherever possible. Initial helpers filled their pockets and muffs with torn undergarments for bandages. With better organization and supplies house to house visits would be made. One volunteer was Dartmouth girl Helen Creighton. She had a car and drove people to aid stations. Later she went to Halifax City Hall and was assigned door to door canvass. Theatre Players at the Academy of Music prepared noon meals for Helen and others. In later life Helen Creighton became internationally known for collecting Nova Scotia folklore, recording words, songs, ghost stories and poems from rural areas.

Daily lists would appear in the newspapers giving names of bodies identified, those injured, persons missing. As time wore on fewer stories appeared of those who were found.

One happy occurrence was duly noted Dec 13, 1917:

'There was joy in the household of Mr. & Mrs. J. Boyle, 133 Creighton Street, yesterday when their four months old baby boy was found. They had diligently searched since the day of the disaster and at last seeing a notice of a baby at the home of Dr. and Mrs. Jakeman they called there and identified the lost infant. They are very grateful to the doctor and his wife for the tender care given to the child.'

---

### News of dead and missing, dealing with local baseball players:

'Local Baseball Athletes Dead and Missing

Denny Sullivan lost his life on Pier 9. He was premier catcher of local Intermediate League.

"Luck" O'Brian the baseball player is among the missing. He was employed as a checker at the Railway.

Carmen McHale star first baseman is missing. He was employed with Canadian Government Railway.

Jack Stokes is also among the missing. He is well remembered as one of the leading spirits of the Saint Joseph's Society and was first baseman of the club for five years.'

**There was also the task of burying the dead:**

On the 17th of December the city would attend the services to bury large numbers of dead.

There would be one service for non Catholic and another for those identified as Catholic. The services were held on snow covered ground in a bright winter sunshine with blue sky. The caskets were brought from the basement of Chebucto School by soldiers and included 2 rows of white caskets, the remains of children, some buried together just as they had been found. Another public service would be held 5 days later on December 22, another on December 24. One of those witnessing the funerals was student Thomas Raddall who had been responsible for escorting soldiers through the school to set up the morgue. He helped

Protestant funeral at Chebucto School, Archbishop Worrell, Church of England and Salvation Army Officers officiate with other Protestant clergy.

Catholic funeral mass at Chebucto School, Father McManus and Father Grey officiating.

The band of the 66th Princess Louise Fusiliers performs next to the platform erected for the officiating clergy.

Loading caskets on truck for burial at cemeteries.

to bring water from neighbouring houses on Chebucto Road to use in the work of preparing the dead for the long lines of people searching for friends and family. Thomas Raddall would later write of the explosion in one of his many books.

Halifax did not have time to linger over the many funerals, that continued into 1918, for the task of taking care of the wounded was great. Time was taken, however, to thank the rescuers and to inform others of the needs of Halifax citizens.

Mother Mary Berchmans, Mother Superior of the Sisters of Charity of Halifax.

A long letter written by the Mother Superior of the Sisters of Charity provides accurate detail of the situation soon after the event. It read in part:

'Mount St. Vincent, Rockingham, N.S.

Dec. 18, 1917

My dear Sisters:
…The explosion, as you know, occurred at five minutes past nine, A. M. (On the 6th. Inst.) And the destruction which in one moment was done to life and property, and the suffering caused by injuries cannot, and probably, never will be estimated.

At the Mount…. Our Pupils acted most satisfactorily, and we are proud of their conduct…the large girls…forgot their wounds, in their desire to help others. And notwithstanding the cold…some of them took off their sweaters to wrap them around the shivering little bodies of the children from outside who, with their parents, rushed in to us for help and protection.

Our Infirmarians and Nurses had scarcely begun the binding and dressing of wounds when some of them were required to turn their attention to more urgent needs. The first to appear on the scene was a soldier drenched in blood. Then followed several from the neighbourhood, some of whom were in a very sad plight. Others belonged to the City. These had been picked up on the road by men in their Autos and brought to us. …The Cottage…is in the possession of a family and we still have a whole family on the ground floor of the South Wing and several orphaned children….

Some of the Sisters found cuts in their clothing and bits of glass lodged next to their persons, and even in their shoes; yet they were not hurt. Those who were in the Community Room were enveloped in a shower of flying glass. Only one was cut, and then slightly. Yet that glass flew in myriads of sword-shaped pieces in all directions, and with such force as to stick in the doors of the Chapel Tribunes, twenty-five feet away….The injuries received, in view of the terrible accident, were indeed few and light. The Sisters who were cut about the head and eyes are rapidly getting better.

A few minutes after the explosion the Sisters were brushing up the broken glass and picking up debris. Some were on top of step-ladders nailing blankets and quilts to the open windows. You can scarcely imagine what it meant to have nearly all the windows of such an establishment as this so completely broken—scarcely a particle of glass remaining in the sashes.

…it often happened that as soon as a window was blocked, the wind threw it open again. … A couple of hours after the explosion an order was sent to the Rockingham people to take to the woods, as another, and more serious explosion was to be momentarily expected. …For a time the fire was making such headway in the direction of the Magazines that it appeared quite impossible to subdue it. It was the flooding of the Magazines that saved the City….Many were the Rosaries said and the promises made during that short exile for the deliverance of the City from this new peril. …

Saint Joseph's Convent, southeast corner of Gottingen and Kaye Streets.

St. Joseph's Church, School and Convent are a mass of ruins… St. Joseph's Convent which was just paid for…not even possible to recover such things as mattresses and provisions from the wreck…Yet St. Joseph's School was a mercy to the majority of the children attending it, for, had it not been in session, most of them would have been killed in their homes… One of the Sisters in the Convent, and three in the School, were considerably injured…. It was at first feared that Sister Rita would lose her vision but better hopes are now entertained of her case….

At the Oxford Street School there was less injury. All the children left the School unharmed….

At St. Patrick's no loss of life has been reported. Our Convent there is very much damaged… Perhaps the least damaged of our Houses are St. Teresa's Home and St. Mary's…The Home of the Guardian Angel is badly injured… Seventy-two Babies and the Sisters are huddled together in one large room. The Orphanage suffers principally on account of broken glass.

When the second explosion was feared, all the people in the City were ordered out on the Common… The Sisters attached to the Infirmary, of course, remained at their posts….

To render the situation still more painful and difficult a war ship arrived laden with wounded soldiers…. This meant the removal of our suffering people from the Military Hospitals….

Mount Saint Vincent Motherhouse, College and Academy.

The suffering of mind and body occasioned by the explosion baffles all attempts at description.... Whole families perished together. Fifty-five men who were employed in the Richmond Iron Foundry (Hillis & Sons) were all killed. ...Frank Hillis, with whom the Community has done business for so many years—one of the Firm, was among the number. His brother James, wife and child, are also killed....

Halifax has received many consolations and generous help in its hour of sorrow and distress. No words can sufficiently praise the prompt and effectual relief offered by the United States. Our Doctors and Nurses were saved from collapse by the timely arrival of the Boston Physicians and Nurses, all of whom are doing a mighty work in the various Hospitals.

Another glance at Mount St. Vincent before finishing.... Large sections of ceiling and walls are stripped of plaster.... If you could see us when congregated for Mass you would be reminded of the Catacombs and the first Christians.... the Sisters wore their cloaks and the wraps they had in their possession.... Woolen hoods are very much in the fashion. Our Furnaces have been kept going to the utmost of their capacity, but when the weather is cold it is like trying to heat the outdoors....

It was such a merciful dispensation of Divine Providence that our Electric Plant Cooking Apparatus, and Furnaces were not thrown out of order....

Asking you again to pray most fervently, and offer many good works for our present needs, and begging our Divine Lord to bless abundantly the efforts of each dear Sister,

Mother M. Berchmans'

Campbell Road—top left of photo is the ruined Hillis Foundry. *Halifax Herald*—'The bodies of Frank Hillis and Harvey Saunders have been discovered buried in the fallen cement of Hillis Foundry. Tho partially crushed they were easily recognizable the faces being only slightly injured. It is supposed that Mr. Hillis who was early at work that morning had seen the fire and watched it from across the road. He and Mr. Saunders were just entering the office door when the explosion occurred which instantly killed them.' The funeral notice: 'Hillis The funeral of Frank D. Hillis will be held from his late residence Waterloo Street, Thursday Morning (private) internment Fairview Cemetery.'

The Sisters of Charity were certainly not the only religious group to reach out to Halifax but their number had a valuable impact on the city. Indeed church groups would work together, some for the first time.

A notice appeared Dec. 21, for the Clerical Relief Organization:

'A meeting of all Clergy of the City is called for this morning in the McCurdy Building 10 o'clock. Clare Worrell convenor of Executive.'

From the *Christian Science Monitor*:

'The response of the United Kingdom and of the Dominions of the British Empire thru-out the earth will be of the kind with that of the United States and its possessions...Halifax will Rise Again. In the hour of the city's trial it will find solace in the thought that friends have arisen for it everywhere.'

Christian Scientists contributed both from the local church and the Mother Church, Boston. Boston Christian Scientist Halifax Relief Committee raised $10,000 and raced a specially chartered train with workers and supplies to Halifax.

'It was decided that a resolution of Appreciation should be prepared and forwarded to the Mother Church First Church of Christ Scientist, Boston and a copy of same should be incorporated in the Minutes'—Halifax Relief Committee. Dec 1917

The Salvation Army response:

A cable from General William Bromwell Booth, London: 'Express sympathy with government and people in the appalling disaster at Halifax. Can we assist? Rely on us. God Bless the bereaved.' $5,000 for relief was cabled.

Commander Eva Booth, Salvation Army, United States, sent $500 with remembrance of many visits to Halifax. The Salvation Army of Western Canada sent $1,000. Other monies would be sent. All officers who could left their corps for Halifax, 22 arrived from Nova Scotia and New Brunswick, 13 from Toronto and Eastern Ontario. 2,500 copies of the 10 cent Christmas number of the *War Cry* were given to patients in hospitals. The Fraser Harris Report on the Salvation Army:

'The Infant's Home on Tower Road did quite useful work at the time of the disaster. For instance, it took in two unknown baby boys on December 8th, both of whom within a few days were claimed by their respective fathers. An unknown baby girl brought in on December 14th was claimed by her father on the same day. Up to December 21st, four children were born in the Home, two boys and one girl, all of whom lived, and one child born prematurely, which died the next day.'

**News of the disaster was far reaching:**

A Holland American Line Ship had been in Bedford Basin awaiting clearance and its ships' press put out a story on December 6 of the events of that day to the 750 passengers onboard, none of whom suffered any injury. Later the following article appeared in world newspapers:

'Reuters Dec. 28 1917
CARRIED SCARS OF HALIFAX EXPLOSION
ROTTERDAM—December 28—

The Dutch steamer Neiuw Amsterdam, with a cargo for Belgium relief passed the Hook of Holland at noon today bound for Rotterdam. The arrival of the Nieuw Amsterdam was an event of almost national importance. Crowds of persons came from all parts of the country and thousands cheered themselves hoarse when the weather beaten liner came in showing scars of the Halifax explosion. ...'

From the newspapers:

'The Red Cross had been welcoming back thousands of soldiers along the docks of Halifax and while maintaining this took on relief work.' 'Representatives of American and Canadian Red Cross Speak of Their High Appreciation of the Local Branch.'

From the Fraser Harris Report:

'Very prominent in their services to the sufferers from the Halifax catastrophe were the nurses, both those on duty at the time and those who came from far and near... nursing sisters of the C.A.M.C. who were on duty on the morning of the 6th in the various military hospitals continued at their posts during the very trying first three days with a quiet devotion to duty which it would be an impertinence to praise. As members of the army of the Empire they gave of their best as though it was part of their daily routine. Equally devoted were the dedicated non military nurses on the staffs of the various hospitals that morning.

No unstinted praise must be meted out to the drivers and other personnel of the military and naval ambulances, which were so continuously requisitioned, not only during the first few days after the explosion, but for many weeks afterwards.'

Daily life in 1917 included animals:

The war was one fought on horseback and soldiers would patrol Halifax after the explosion.

Many horses died on the docks or were found with destroyed delivery wagons. Hens, chickens, and domestic animals ran loose. A variety of action had to be taken and notices would appear in the newspapers.

Sailors from USS *Old Colony* had to shoot 6 injured horses.

'150 head of cattle could be cared for at Exhibition Grounds'

New York SPCA had to search and destroy dogs that were in ruined areas foraging for any type of food source. Massachusetts SPCA arrived Dec. 14 and destroyed 14 horses, dogs and cats injured in blast. Massachusetts SPCA gave $1,000 for animal relief.

In Halifax newspapers notices concerning animals appeared:

'The dog belonging to the Captain of *Imo* had to be shot—would not allow men in cabin of ship.'

'A central stable for horses and sleighs was established for relief work.'

Dec. 18 notice: 'Animal Relief Committee ... established in Juvenile Court Building, Argyle and Prince send all information regarding animals missing and all needing shelter, food and veterinary treatment, persons ready to take dogs or other pet animals, also those having barns or buildings ready to be used as shelters. R.H. Murray Chairman'

'M. Driscoll whose child was killed, is making every effort to locate the little one's pet dog, a Boston terrier, answering to the name of Otto and the Animal Relief Committee is co-operating with him in the search.'

Aged 10 at the time of the explosion, Sherman Hubley, of Kane Street would later recall that his father was upset their Jersey Cow was killed by flying metal. The 2 horses were OK. Sherman lived on the property until his death in 1996.

Soldiers on horseback patrolled 20—40 miles a day to prevent looting. In this photo a mounted soldier poses outside the ruins of Oland's Brewery, Agricola Street.

**For a city needing supplies train car loads would arrive along with cash donations:**

Quaker Oats Company—100 cases rolled oats
Mount Royal Milling, Montreal—10,000 pounds rice
Dominion Molasses Co., Halifax—250 cases molasses
Atlantic Sugar Co. St. John—150 cases sugar
Chase & Sanborn Co., Montreal—500 packages of coffee
Christie Brown Co. Ltd., Toronto—200 boxes of biscuits
Citizens of Sydney Mines—13 boxes of foodstuffs
Bovril Ltd., Montreal—6 dozen cases Bovril
Robin Hood Flour Mills, Montreal—400 bags flour
Kellogg's Toasted Corn Flakes Co.—50 cases Corn Flakes
Boyd Shoe and Rubber Co. Seattle, Wash.—1 box of supplies

Miss Kathleen Ewing, Enfield, Mass.—toys and games
Captain, Officers and staff CS Restorer, Charleston, Washington State, 158.00
Mr. Grieggs, Bank of New York, NY, 1,000.00
Collection, First National Bank, Wyoming, 144.50
H. Choate and family, Winona, Minnesota, 100.00
Rear Admiral & Mrs. E. Chambers, Sydney [they had moved from Halifax], 200.00
Albany Chamber of Commerce, New York, 2,000.00
The Misses Mary and Elizabeth Quinn, Ramsey, N. J., 10.00
Two sailors SS Sercoop, 2.00
Frederica Louisa Scott, Chicago, Illinois, 1.00
Dr. Albert A. Wells, Ashville North Carolina, 10.00

Children at Christmas time in Columbus Hall, a photograph that appeared in the *Halifax Herald*, December 1917. 'Columbus Hall the handsome headquarters of the Knights of Columbus, 63 Hollis Street has been very generously used as a place of shelter, irrespective of religious denomination to those who have a need.' The Knights of Columbus offered room to accommodate 150 people in emergency shelter.

Chapter 10

# WHAT OF THE CHILDREN?
# CHRISTMAS 1917

*'To the Superintendent of schools*

*Enclosed please find a check for $100 the donation of the pupils at 188B to the suffering children at Halifax. The pupils of 188B are very poor. They have felt the pangs of suffering and want. Their deepest sympathies are with the children of Halifax. They regret they cannot give more at this time. Hoping that the days of a just peace are not far distant.*

*Edward Mandel*
*Principal PS 188B Manhattan'*
This letter appeared January 4, 1918, in Halifax newspapers.

**Children carrying grocery orders for their families outside the North Park Street door of the Armouries.**

In the files of the State House Archives in Boston there is mention in 1913 that the Government of the Dominion of Canada is spending so much on new shipping terminals in Halifax that those port improvements would be a threat to the Port of Boston. Indeed the blasting through rock in Halifax for the new terminals was, at first, thought by some in the Southend of the City to be the cause of their broken windows on Dec 6, 1917.

The State House files also reveal the story of the help sent Halifax. There were many who sent notes requesting information on family and friends. There is a large correspondence regarding fundraising and there are letters offering employment, such as this one:

'Dec 12/17
Henry B. Endicott
Halifax Relief Comm.
Dear Sir:
We could give a good home and moderate wages to a Protestant woman of good family, to do general house work. Want one that is cheerful, neat and clean,—one that we could consider one of the family.

If satisfactory could give a permanent position. Family consists of middle aged business man and his wife. We live in a comfortable home in a pretty village in the vicinity of Boston.

Address, A. F., Pearl St., Stoughton, Mass'

Many Haligonians would seek employment in the 'Boston States' because of lost industry in Halifax, continuing the close ties that had started before the Revolutionary War.

Snow covers the interior of the tailoring department of Clayton and Sons, a clothing factory on Barrington Street.

On Dec. 6 thoughts of the work place would be put on hold as people tried to cope. At Cogswell Military Hospital alone over 500 injured were treated in 24 hours. So many mild cases of shell shock were observed that these were not reported on hospital charts.

As local doctors and ships' doctors tried to save lives they were affected by the dying. So too the sailors of the USS *Old Colony* who reported 'children died in their arms muttering parents' names or their own pet names.'

The world had heard many shocking stories during World War I. The war in Europe had meant hardship and death for children but in Halifax over 400 children under 14 years of age were killed and thousands of others were injured and left homeless in one day. Newspapers, around the world wrongly assumed children would be in school on a

Thursday morning. With different starting times in winter many children were not yet at their desks. Few of the children attending Saint Joseph's School and Richmond School actually died in the buildings. Many children died in their family home, others had run to see the excitement of a ship on fire. Many Catholic boys of the Northend died because they did not have to attend school until the afternoon, the girls were using the school in the mornings that week. One building where many children died was the Protestant Orphanage on Veith Street. The Matron had gathered the children in the basement of the building on hearing the first minor explosions; she thought the city was being bombed. Matron Mary Knaut, Miss Ethel Mary Melvin, assistant matron and 27 children were killed when the orphanage collapsed and burned.

Protestant Orphanage gates, Barrington Street remained the only trace of the institution.

The concern for children was a motivation of much relief effort, for example:

Dec 13— On the afternoon before the Massachusetts State Guard left Halifax, Major Baker, Captain Nathaniel Morse and Captain Lapham assumed the role of Santa Claus and carried to the children in hospital a generous contribution of toys.

Dec 14—American Red Cross Society sent letter to Mrs. William Dennis, Halifax, stating their desire to send certain presents to homeless children for Christmas.

Dec 14—'From a student Lytton Avenue School, Palo Alto, California

To the Mayor of Halifax

My Dear Mr. Mayor—I sell newspapers before and after school. One evening I read of the dreadful disaster that nearly destroyed Halifax. I felt very sorry when I thought of the people without homes. The next day I asked our school principal if the children might not help some of the homeless children of Halifax. She is sending the money to you. I hope it will help you some.

Yours truly,

Lewis Hickey

6A student'

[Amount from students, sent by Principal, was $19.00]

Concern for children took many forms including offers of adoption. From the file, State House Archives, Boston:

'Pawtucket, R.I.

Dec. 12, 1917

A.C. Ratchesky.

Dear Sir,

I have read in the Boston Post also in the Pawtucket Times of little children who have been left without parents. Now if you have a nice child about 6 or 8 I should be very glad to give them a good home as I have none of my own. I would prefer a girl. Will you please let me know.

Yours very truely.

Mrs. H. F. E.

129 Dunnell Av.

Pawt. R.I.'

The reply:

'December 19, 1917.

Dear Madam:...

Your generous offer is much appreciated. However, we are unable to say now whether there will be any children available as the disposition in Halifax seems to be to take care of those cases themselves if possible....'

Along with the letters received in Boston, the Children's Aid Society in Halifax received over 450 inquiries. 112 requests came from the United States. Many wrote of having given up a son for the war.

From the Children's Aid Society records:

South Dakota—Dec 15, 1917:

'I have just been reading in the Sault City Journal on where there were 200 children left orphans. We have been trying to get two or three nice little children that are homeless. We would give them a good home here in South Dakota on a ranch.'

Idaho—Dec 16, 1917:

'I was reading of the horror of your town I can't come to do anything as I am a widow with three boys and live on a farm but I will take one of the orphans to care for if you will let me have a small boy or baby girl that is homeless. I will be willing to adopt it or take it until you know for sure that it is an orphan. I can do that much and will be very glad to get a little girl my children are all boys and all go to school so hope to hear soon.'

Tennessee—Dec 23, 1917:

'Please, about sending me those negro girls, I presume there are negro children in Halifax but I have no idea how many, and I wanted to help them so they's be apt to be the last ones to be permanently provided for. If you have some promising white women who are destitute and are anxious for a good Christian education let me know. I can plan to take care of them too.' Steele Home of Needy Children, Mrs. A.S. Steele Founder and Manager.

From Anto Chico, New Mexico: there was a letter in Spanish from a gentleman to his Congressman in Washington offering to adopt one of the Halifax children. The Congressmen forwarded the letter.

Another couple wanted a boy or girl 'strong and healthy of good description but not with red hair.'

Other letters spoke of how they would try to do well by the children 'a boy 10-15…coming of his own free will.'

One couple, a doctor and his wife in Nebraska, thinking of the future, 'wanting a boy who could take up medicine and give relief to his practice.'

The answer that Nova Scotia would look after all children disappointed many.


The Children's Committee of the relief effort would place daily ads in the newspapers for information on 'Missing Children:'

'Walsh Freddie Two years. Last seen at Armouries. Sister fainted and boy was taken from her then.

Vaughn Bernard 4 years dark might call for Popsy.

Hinch 2 years dark hair, black eyes, blue mark across nose, fingers on one hand slightly bent, says Daddy Ned or Mommy dear

Mondy Ruth 1 year brown grey eyes, light brown hair, inclined to be curley. Fully dressed, point broke off front tooth, mole on back. Might call for Jean or Marion sisters or brother William.

Sitland Pearl 10 probably in nightdress, Earl 6 dressed for school in suit, short pants, Jimmie between 3-4, Joseph between 2-3, Ralph 7-8 months no teeth.

Elizabeth 5 years fair blue eyes Dutch cut. Wearing blue check rompers No.12, was from Protestant Orphanage. A little boy at Infirmary says he saw this child after explosion with his little sister who is now at the IODE home.

MacKinnon Donald 13 months large for his age Teeth 3 above 2 below. Light brown Hair, grey blue eyes not able to walk but crawled around and could stand with chair, Quiet but hearty boisterous laugh when amused.'

Some children were listed as found but not claimed:

'Boy about 2 years fair hair blue eyes calls himself Gordy when shown pictures of man in uniform.

Boy about 3 years. Supposed to be Austin, Arseneau or Archer. Speaks of sister, playmate Jimmie. Says Winnie took him to church. Speaks very indistinctly.'

## Some donations specifically given for the relief of children:

As recorded by Halifax Relief Committee in their ledgers:
[Funds converted to Canadian money—In 1917 $26 a week was a good pay.]
Mrs. Schopp, Richmond, Virginia, 70.00
A friend, Wilmington, Delaware, 2.00
Rev. and Mrs. Harris, Fulton, Calif. 5.00
Mrs. W.C. Roso, Brooklyn, Mass. 123.45
Miss E.E. Broadhead, East Marish Chuck, PA. 5.00
Wm. Fraser Minneapolis, Minnesota, 25.00
The Life Underwriters Association of New York City, 262.50
Pupils Public School, 46 Rue Camleon, Paris, France, 3.50
Canadian Club New York, NY, 8,000
People of Hudson Bay Co. James Bay, Canada, 300.00
Lake Francis Drama Club, Lake Francis, Manitoba, 42.00
#1 Girl Guides, Windsor, Ontario, 2.50
Apr. 30, 1918 Soldiers Wives Club Red Deer, Alberta, 50.00
Women's Patriotic Club, Granelbury Saskatchewan, 150.00
Girls Glee Club Sherbrooke Quebec, 129.50
July 31, 1918 Children of British Guiana, 211.70

Soon after the sad news of dead and missing children started appearing, it was announced on Dec. 15th that there was an outbreak of diphtheria in the city. Vast majority of cases would have been children under age of 10 but due to the crowded conditions older children and adults were not exempt. Patients would suffer headaches, malaise, fever, sore throat, difficulty breathing and then death. There was a diphtheria antitoxin that had been developed in 1894 but it took time to arrange for the medications. Medical authorities thus had one more challenge to face in treating thousands of injured children.

The School for the Blind was turned into a hospital. Newly blind children were welcomed by long term students. Good medical care prevented further injury and reduced numbers of permanently impaired.

In a letter to the VON from Sir Frederick Fraser, he said, 'Before you leave Halifax I desire to express to you, on behalf of myself and the committee for the Halifax Blind Relief Work, our very sincere and grateful thanks for all the help given us through the Victorian Order of Nurses and for the inspiration they have been in the prevention of unnecessary blindness in Halifax.'

Sir Frederick Fraser brought to the attention of the Massachusetts Relief Committee the need for immediate care and the education of those visually impaired by the explosion. The committee set aside $25,000 for this purpose. Archibald MacMechan, official historian of the disaster, recorded in his personal journal attending on Feb. 18, 1918 Washington's Birthday party, at the School for the Blind, given to recognize U.S. helpers.

With hundreds of eye injuries reported in newspapers, money was sent to the Halifax Relief Committee—directed to the care of the Blind. This was duly noted in Committee accounts:

Jan. 2, 1918 Mr. & Mrs. Morrison, Berkeley, Calif., USA, $20.00
Miss A. E. Smith, Coronado Beach, Calif., USA, 61.94
A friend, Spokane, Wash., USA, 5.00
Union Grove & Paris Corners, ME Churches, Wisconsin, USA, 36.80
Jan. 16, Pupils of Miss V.L. Gordon, Nanaimo, BC, Canada, 3.26
June 27, 1918 Citizens of Kingston, Jamaica, 150.00

The Halifax Blind Relief Committee also gratefully accepted donations directed through Sir Frederick Fraser [known as the Blind Knight], School for Blind, Halifax including:

J.W. Hollenback, Wilkes-Barra, Pa, $ 10.00,
Miss Mary E. Deckman, Connecticut, 100.00
Woman's Club, NY Association for Blind, 10.00,
F.L. Franklin, Warren, Ohio, 10.00
Hebrew Association for Blind, New York, 5.00
Hiram Sibley, Rochester, NY, 500.00
Proceeds of Pie and Basket Social, Coles Island, NB, 71.10
Mrs. A.J. MacNab, Thompson, Nevada, 50.00

Looking east from Tower Road to School for the Blind. There were 142 students enrolled in the school in 1917. New programmes would be established for the large number of adults blinded by the explosion.

As Christmas grew closer, gifts and donations arrived for Halifax children:

Dec 18—Mt. Pleasant Methodist Church, Vancouver 'Christmas Cheer for Halifax Children' $130.00

Mrs. George Ellsworth Braintree Mass., Candles for Children's Christmas Treat

St. Andrews Kirk, Chatham Ont., clothes and toys

Livingston Park Seminary, Rochester, N.Y., Supplies en route

Dec. 20—Boys of Presbyterian Sunday School Barrie, Ontario, Mitts for Boys in Halifax

Unitarian Sunday School, Franklin, NH, Toys

Two young girls put in a claim to the Relief Committee for 'dollies killed in the Explosion.' Office staff took up a collection to buy them new dolls.

Dec. 21, 1917—Notice in *Halifax Herald*:

'Santa Claus Limited, organized last night to provide Christmas Cheer for 10,000 homeless children, needs workers and automobiles WILL YOU HELP?'

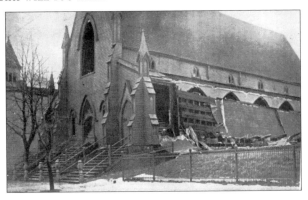

**Above: Saint John's Presbyterian Church, Brunswick Street, was so damaged the congregation rebuilt on Windsor Street.**

**Left: The only sport in Halifax during reconstruction as most recreation buildings were destroyed or heavily damaged.**

Children who had heard so much of war thought other places in Nova Scotia might also have been under attack. In the records of the Relief Committee is a story of a 9 year old girl from Halifax on her way by train to family in Toronto. A reporter let her use his typewriter for a letter to Santa Claus:

'Dear Santa Claus

I hope you escaped all explosions and are safe. I wish you a merry Christmas.

Your friend

Juanita Mallison'

Donations poured in as appeals were made; not all as strongly worded as this notice from the newspaper in Colorado Springs, U.S.A.:

'REMEMBER HALIFAX!

Let us pack a box for Halifax. Let us prove that the great heart of Colorado Springs beats in sympathy with the stricken people of the north.

Let us show them that we are real neighbors; that America is a true friend!

…Winter is upon them—winter with its biting winds, swirling snow and freezing cold. It finds thousands of them homeless, clothesless, foodless. It finds families broken up by death in its most fearful and sudden coming. It finds hearts aching and lives shadowed with bitter sorrow.

It finds poor widows with small children crying for something to eat and the warmth of the houses which were theirs and which now are heaps of blackened wreckage.

We must give them fuel and food, medicine and clothing to keep them alive, and other things to comfort and cheer. And we must not forget the children. Santa Claus must visit every home in Halifax. That will be our Christmas gift to Halifax.'

## Many buildings served the needs of the survivors and their rescuers:

At the Citadel fortress many received aid and shelter. Halifax Dispensary, Brunswick St. distributed relief and housed people. Rockhead prison was used for housing and medical aid.

Pine Hill Divinity College used as hospital for citizens and soldiers, it was already being used for convalescing military. St. Paul's Hall on Argyle St. served 10,000 meals in December and gave shelter as well. 50 women and children were sheltered in the Masonic Building, Barrington St.. The City Home on South St., theatres and amusement halls also gave shelter.

Not long after the disaster, Mr. and Mrs. H.M. Rosenberg of Crichton Ave., Dartmouth, generously offered the use of their residence as an emergency hospital of thirty beds. The Medical Relief Committee gladly accepted the offer.

Crowds gather outside the Gottingen Street door of Alexander McKay School, for relief supplies.

Mailboxes were gathered from devastated Richmond District. As Christmas approached small openings were cut in the planking of boarded up storefronts to let people see that businesses were open. In this photo it can be seen that a storm window was used sideways to suit the owner's purpose. This building was the location of the Victoria School of Art and Design. It would be many months before Halifax had enough glass to replace all the broken windows.

Chapter 11

# Entering 1918

*'Owing to the terrible disaster which has befallen Halifax with its awful loss of life and destruction of property, His Honour the Lieutenant Governor has decided NOT to hold the usual New Year's Day Levee.*
*By Order,*
*John Hicks, Private Secretary'*

A notice that appeared in all Halifax newspapers,
in the last week of December 1917.

The Manual Training School on Cunard St. was the first school to open near the Richmond District.

Halifax had Christmas as best it could. The babies born would be considered to have truly been 'born in a manger' due to the rough conditions in the city. People would gather at Christian services in boarded up churches, theatres, amusement halls, in dining rooms, wherever space could by found. Citizens might give praise for those who had survived but they would do it cold, somewhat hungry, and sad from their losses.

Another Sister of Charity was to write of her experiences. Unfortunately her name is not with her words at the Mount Saint Vincent Archives. She was at Saint Patrick's School and Convent and is possibly Sister Mary Michael who is mentioned in Sister Julia Teresa's account. Her words provide a summary of what had happened. In writing on Dec. 28, 1917 she apologizes for delay in reply to request for

information and expresses that her personal experience was mild compared to the others. It is interesting she makes no mention of Christmas. Sister at the end of her letter mentions the loss of possessions, thoughts common to many in disaster. Her letter reads in part:

'Halifax, N.S.
Dec. 28, 1917
My first thought…was of "the crack of doom"; my second…that we were being bombarded from the air, or shelled from the sea. I called, "Run to the basement". The children heard only "Run"…. There was no screaming, just a blind drive without protection thru a thick storm of crashing glass, plaster, blackboards, doors and statuary.

The explosion was over before we were down stairs, but the continuous falling of large pieces of furniture prolonged the impression that some sort of attack was still in progress. After a few moments we went to the yard… We took to the convent those seriously cut and sent to their homes all needing less attention. …

We had scarcely reached the house when soldiers rushed thru the city with the warning that another explosion was expected to follow and that the people were ordered to seek the nearest places of safety; the Common, Citadel Hill and the Park, as the houses would undoubtedly succumb to this second shock. The entire surviving population of the North End, therefore, quickly went to the Common.

It was an assembly to be remembered, and to a reflective mind offered a faint suggestion of the great final gathering. There were the infants of the Foundling Asylum, each borne lovingly in the arms of the sisters or of the soldiers who had come to their rescue; the panic stricken children from the Institute for the Deaf… the aged, the sick, the dying; priests, laity; Catholic, Protestant; rich and poor; every class distinction nullified, every antipathy forgotten, in the wave of sympathy and fear which united all hearts. There were births and deaths in these open places of refuge during that horrible hour of suspense….

… The floors of wards and corridors in Camp Hill, the hospital to which I went, were so closely packed that it was almost impossible to pass between the bodies…. Death was here in various forms; some had been drowned by the great waves from the parted waters; some burned by the powder and pitch; some mangled by splintered glass, or wounded by large pieces of iron from the ship. … One mother seeking her little boy found him with both eyes blown out. His first words as he took her hand were, "Mama, it is night".

We found two of our sisters among the wounded. They had been rescued from St. Joseph's School and, in the confusion, carried to this hospital, instead of to our own….

The Orphanage on Quinpool Road was badly shattered and many of the orphans were cut, but there was not loss of life. The house was soon made ready for the many, whose parents were lost. Twenty-six were received a few days after the tragedy, when the hospitals were first relieved; and since, each day finds the number increasing.

The Foundling Asylum…. Two were lost in the crowd on the Common. One, James McGee, had for two days a visit with a lady who had formerly been a pupil of the Sisters. The similarity of "Shamie's" devotions with those which she had herself learned in youth, gave her the necessary clue to his home…. As to the other, there has appeared in the Halifax papers every night since December 6 the following announcement under the long, long column, Children Lost; Dominic —(Austrian child)—Belongs to Home of Guardian Angel; very fair, blue eyes….

In St. Theresa's Home… Sick from the hospitals have now been received there in connection with the Infirmary. The sisters in these institutions were assisted by the Rhode Island Unit during the two weeks following the Explosion. I wish you could hear the blessing which the poor and suffering invoke on the Americans. Surely, the United States is the great, warm heart of the world. On the morning after the arrival of the First Relief Train from the States, I went in the hospital to a poor man whose eyes had been terribly injured. He has been in despair; now, he grasped my hand saying, "Sister, I am going to be all right. There's a Yankee nurse looking after me, and, I tell you, she knows her business". This was the beginning of an endless chain of gratitude….

The greatest loss to the Community is the enormous amount of damage to our Mother House, Mt. St. Vincent…. Every window was broken, some of them old and of stained glass of great value. Pictures and statues were destroyed—the old treasures that mean history to a community. Loyal, loving gifts! All are gone—the priceless mementoes of the friends who struggled with or for us in the days of long ago….

Farewell'

The work of rehabilitation would take years and for many Haligonians life would never return to 'normal.' The federal election in Halifax was postponed until January. It was announced due to the destruction of the buildings, the Exhibition would not be held in 1918.

Decisions also had to be made about schools. Some schools were destroyed, others used for relief work needed repair. When the schools did re-open, they were shared on shifts. Southend and Central children went in the mornings, Northend children attended in the afternoons. It would take time to return to the usual neighbourhood classes. Some students would have to leave school to help earn an income for families trying to restore their lives.

Dalhousie University was the first of the colleges to place notices of reopening. Their notice announced the scheduled date would be January 3rd at 9am, with mention that special examinations would be held immediately and Christmas exams by the end of January.

The Dalhousie students would write with humour in their newspaper the *Gazette*: 'Not even TNT could Stop Exams.'

'The faculty, always so tenderly considerate of the students, felt that, in spite of the catastrophe, it would be shameful to deprive them of the Christmas examinations, and so on the 21st of January, they played Santa Claus by presenting us with a series of one hour quizzes. Then, lest we grow blasé with inaction, they ordained that lectures should continue through the examination period. Great was the

Broken windows, Dalhousie Science Building in southend Halifax. 'So intense was the explosion that windows did not fall out but were broken into pieces from dust to the size of your finger and flung about like snow or hail so that even in this area of the City there are people cut.'—Stanley MacKenzie, President of Dalhousie.

The MacDonald Library at Dalhousie. Many of the students
were serving overseas so enrollment was reduced. Injuries
were cuts and bruises, one student lost an eye.

gnashing of teeth among the afflicted as the explosion had blown every molecule of knowledge out of many a normally near vacuum.'

Despite feeling overworked, the students, along with their other relief efforts raised $60.55 to give to Sir Frederick Fraser for his work with the newly blinded.

To pay for some of the damage to Dalhousie buildings, President MacKenzie approached Mr. Andrew Carnegie of the United States who previously contributed $40,000 to the construction of the Science Building. Opened February 11, 1915, the Science Building had been named the Carnegie Peace Memorial Building to signify 100 years of peace between Canada and the United States.

President MacKenzie received a telegram stating that the Carnegie Corporation would pay the costs of damage to all the buildings of Dalhousie whatever they might be. The costs of repair were over $20,000 all of which were paid for by Mr. Carnegie.

The university's reply on January 14, 1918, read in part:

'To…Carnegie Corporation of New York,

Fifth Ave. New York City

…Appreciated friendly and gracious spirit in which the gift was made. The spontaneous and instantaneous outpouring of assistance and comfort and sympathy which reached Halifax from the American people is superb and has made it impossible to put adequately in words what we have felt about it but it has established a bond of union between the people of this part of the world and those on your side of the line which will defy breaking.

Faithfully yours

President Dalhousie Stanley MacKenzie'

**From Halifax newspapers:**

'Jan. 3, 1918: Captain A.E. Seaman injured in the explosion has returned to his home in Pugwash accompanied by his wife and daughter Ida who were also slightly injured.'

'In the YMCA hospital in one ward is a mother who it is believed is totally blinded; in another is her husband who has lost the sight in one eye and in another her little daughter both of whose eyes had to be removed. A few days ago following the birth of her baby, the mother said that she thought she could ever so faintly see the little newcomer and it is the hope of the doctors that her sight might be restored.'

'January 4, 1918—Lost an eye: The many friends of Miss Mary Mulcahy nurse at the Infectious Diseases Hospital will regret that the injuries to her eye caused by the explosion, were so severe that it necessitates its removal.'

'Will be ready Sunday: The basement of Saint Patrick's Church is being put in shape for holding services and will probably be ready for Sunday's Masses.'

St. George's Church (left) and St. Patrick's Church (right) Brunswick Street, were both heavily damaged in the explosion.

At Saint Mary's College, Windsor Street, the Americans led by Dr. Ladd stayed until January 5, 1918, at which time they returned to Boston. Then the Rhode Island Red Cross took over. The hospital with 138 beds would remain open until January 14 when repairs would start for the re-opening of school. Arthur Inglis noted the extended closing:

Arthur, a 21 year old engineering student, was walking along Robie Street from his house just south of the Morris Street Fire Station. He met a friend at the Willow Tree. They noticed smoke in the Northend past the Commons. Next they found that they had been knocked across the street and counted themselves lucky. 'If I had been in school, I might have had broken glass in my eye. The next day there was a terrific snowstorm. The day after that folks from Boston arrived with a whole hospital outfit. They did a marvellous job.' In the optimistic spirit of youth and with no serious injuries in his family Arthur was 'kind of happy there was no school for awhile.'

**American medical personnel posing in front of Saint Mary's College where windows still needed repair. Archbishop McCarthy gave Saint Mary's College gladly as Emergency Hospital. He advised that: '15 Christian Brothers of Ireland in residence would assist or vacate as deemed best.'**

Halifax N.S.
Jan. 3rd 1918
To Messrs McKessen and
Robbins,
Chemist's, New York City

Please accept hearty thanks Medical Relief Committee Halifax for your kind donation of four hundred and forty-eight pounds of chloroform and two hundred and fifty pounds of ether for the use of sufferers in Halifax Disaster. Your generosity greatly appreciated by all. McKelvey Bell Lieut.-Col. Chairman Medical Relief Committee

Mount Saint Vincent Academy would also re-open for students in January. Boston papers had published 'Two Boston Girls Survive.' 'Among the survivors of the Halifax disaster to arrive in Boston on the St. John Express... were Miss Dorothy McKenzie of Roxbury and Miss Katherine White of Dorchester.... The girls were overcome by their terrible experience.'

Katherine White stated: 'The school building shook like a leaf. Every window crumbled. Then came the awful screaming. Men came to us and asked for bandages. We tore up sheets and gave it to them. By that time loads of dying and injured were being brought to us in wagons.'

One of many human interest stories featured in the *Boston Globe*, Saturday, December 8, 1917.

## SURVIVE DISASTER

### Students at Academy Return to Homes

### Misses White and McKenzie Tell of Catastrophe at Halifax

Among the survivors of the Halifax disaster to arrive in Boston on the St. John express at 9.30 last night, were Miss Dorothy McKenzie of 46 Magnolia st. Roxbury, and Miss Katherine C. White of 56 Richfield st. Dorchester. The young women were students at the Academy and College of Mt. St. Vincent's at Rockingham.

MISS KATHERINE WHITE
Of Dorchester. Survivor of Halifax Disaster.

The Board of the Halifax Ladies College, a private girl's school on Barrington Street, gave permission for the building to be used as a hospital; it was taken over by the Maine State Medical Unit.

The girls recorded their response to relief work in the June 1918, *Olla Podriea*, the school magazine:

'The disaster of December the sixth last will always be in our memories. In years to come it may be asked how the H.L.C. and its girls fared at that time.

The College itself became a hospital. It proved itself an asset to the city. The teachers all assigned themselves to some activity and a canvass among the girls shows that they did their "bit" and what is even better did their "best"

The work comprised:—Delivering telegrams

Helping in distribution of clothing at Green Lantern [building] and with Massachusetts Clothing Dept.

Working at Technical College making sheets and bandages

At St. Paul's Hall working in kitchen, serving meals, making up beds.

Filling Christmas Stockings for destitute and sick children.

Collecting toys for "Cousin Peggy" (at Echo office).

Serving tea at Camp Hill Hospital. Helping at the Children's Hospital and washing floors.

Nursing some babies taken to their homes for shelter...

Others who were out of town made flannelette night dresses for the destitute.

Collected Christmas gifts to send to Halifax.

Working in home town to relieve V.A.D.'s for Halifax work.

Visiting Halifax sufferers at the out-of-town emergency hospitals at Truro and New Glasgow and so on.

In replying to the question: "what did you do after the explosion?" —some took it literally and answered with candour:

J said, "Swept up Lockie's room, then packed up my glad rags and scooted."

R said "Swept glass out of hall, then 'beat it' for home."

R said "Waited a *whole* afternoon at the Terminals for a train to take me home."'

The one school not to re-open in Halifax was the Royal Naval College. The escape of the Cadets from serious injury was reported in the *Calgary Daily Herald* Dec. 10, 1917: 'One of the miracles of explo-

DEPARTMENT OF THE NAVAL SERVICE

## ROYAL NAVAL COLLEGE CANADA.

The Royal Naval College is established for the purpose of imparting a complete education in Naval Science.

Graduates are qualified to enter the Imperial or Canadian Services as midshipmen. A Naval career is not compulsory, however. For those who do not wish to enter the Navy the course provides a thorough grounding in Applied Science and is accepted as qualifying for entry as second year students in Canadian Universities.

The scheme of education aims at developing discipline with ability to obey and take charge, a high sense of honour, both physical and mental, a good grounding in Science, Engineering, Mathematics, Navigation, History and Modern Languages, as a basis for general development of further specialization.

Particulars of entry may be obtained on application to the Department of the Naval Service, Ottawa.

Pending erection of buildings to replace those destroyed at the time of the Halifax disaster the Royal Naval College is located at Esquimalt, near Victoria, B.C.                              G. J. DESBARATS,

Deputy Minister of the Naval Service.

Unauthorized Publication of this advertisement will not be paid for.

Ottawa, February 3, 1919.

sion. The youngsters [average age 15]… were watching the fire… from windows. Injuries mostly small cuts… and bruises. Those in residence [of 36 students] Leon Winans, Joseph Terry, Montreal, Arnold Smith, Robert Brett, Toronto, Kenneth MacKenzie, Wakefield, Ont., Harold Pentelow, Guelph, Ont., Wilson Beckles, Windsor, Ont., Cadet

Captain Edward Kingsmill, son of Admiral Kingsmill, R. Orde, Fred Hillard, George Desbarates, Ottawa, Ont., William Holmes, Lindsay Pritchard, Victoria, B.C., Wilfred Richardson, son of Bishop Richardson, Fredericton, George Mills, St. John, N.B., A.C. Lee, Dawson City, Y.T.. Young Orde is wounded in the back while Pentelow is reported as hurt in the eyes.'

For the rest of the term the cadets attended the Royal Military College in Kingston, Ontario where the cost of the course for 3 years was $800 including board, uniform, instructional material and all extras. The next term the naval cadets were moved to British Columbia.

As late as 1921 ads in the *Dalhousie Gazette* for the Royal Naval College stated 'pending erection of buildings to replace those destroyed at the time of the Halifax Disaster the Royal Naval College is located at Esquimalt near Victoria BC.' The College never returned to Halifax.

Out of town colleges offered help: Dr. Cutten, President of Acadia in Wolfville, offered the help of 50 students [including Charles Huggins, 16, a native of Halifax who would later win the Nobel prize for Medicine and teach in Chicago] and a staff engineer to come to the city. The women of Mount Saint Bernard's in Antigonish made fudge for fundraising.

King's College students in their *Kings College Record* of Feb. 1918 would report disappointment that the college buildings [in Windsor, N.S.] were not used for the 'Halifax Sufferers.' However, a number of students 'ventured from Windsor to aid in the relief work. Messrs. Jefferson, Winter, Cribb, Holly and Mr. Gabriel who placed himself and his automobile at the disposal of the transportation committee.' King's College School re-opened January 22 and advertised vacancies for those students whose city schools were closed.

January also saw the first temporary housing built, the Gov. McCall Apartments on the Exhibition Grounds, Almon Street. Mr. A.C. Ratchesky of Massachusetts on visiting stated: 'There has been a wonderful improvement since our visit here shortly after the explosion. Considering the weather conditions that have prevailed the progress has been marvellous and the cosy homes which are now almost ready and a complete one of which we visited today are a credit to the builders and will doubtless be appreciated by the occupants.

We will leave for home on Monday evening and will carry back a report which will surely be pleasing to the people of New England who wish to do all they can for the relief of those who suffered from the awful disaster which fell upon your city.'

Top photo: A new kitchen in the temporary housing on the Exhibition Grounds, Almon St., note the labels are still on the pot and the kettle.

Bottom photo: Gov McCall Apartments; temporary housing for the survivors built with funds sent from the United States.

The relief work and news of disaster victims continued to occupy local newspaper columns:

Jan. 3—Lewis Verner, 24, of crew of Douglas Thomas from Louisbourg, Cape Breton passed away from Explosion injuries at Halifax Infirmary.

Jan. 7—Leo Fultz, altar boy, who served mass for last time on morning of Explosion died in hospital of injuries.

Citizens petitioned city hall to allow pond at Public Gardens to be used for ice skating as Shirley Street rink was damaged in disaster. The Mayflower Curling Rink, where the *Titanic* victims had been laid out in 1912, was also damaged in the explosion.

Other news of the day:

'The King's proclamation calling for a day of prayer was read yesterday in most of the churches of Halifax which were left standing or in fit condition for service after the great disaster.'

'The French Cable Company has made a gift of $4,000 to Halifax Relief'

Village of Bronxville, New York 3 cases of clothes.

Corn Products Company, New York 50 cases Karo Syrup

Messrs. H. J. Heinz Co., $500

'Only 4 days of cold and stormy weather making transportation of coal impossible to make coal famine in Halifax a Reality'

January Donations continued:

'Officers and Crew SS Saranac, $400

Australian Transport Ship Demoathenes, $307.23

Grace Hall Methodist Church, Folkestone, England, 34.

Fashion Jewelry Inc. New York c/o Woods Bros., 10.

Solomon Simon, Philadelphia per Moirs Ltd., 10.

Nurses & Staff Hospital of the Good Samaritan Los Angeles, 35.50

Police Mutual Benefit Dance Victoria BC, 250.

Women Permanent Emergency of Germantown Philadelphia, Pa. clothing and wool.'

Jan. 15—'American Red Cross offices, Keith Building, to close.'

American Red Cross supplies were given to Canadian Red Cross. Principal Sexton of Technical College on Spring Garden Road provided space for 50-60 staff of the Red Cross of which Canadian Commercial Travellers formed a large part. Mr. R.A. Jewkes a druggist from Providence, Rhode Island welcomed a large contribution of drugs from T. Eaton and Co. of Toronto brought by the head of the Drug Department.

View of Technical College Medical Depot, Spring Garden Road. On Dec. 9th, 40 Commercial Travellers arrived to help in rescue work, many stayed into January to distribute medical supplies at the Technical College. On Dec. 14th, thanks was given to Commercial Travellers Association for their assistance, in the Board of Trade Rooms

H.H. Marshall offered to sell the Relief Committee commemorative postcard booklets to send to donors. The committee turned down this expense. [Postcards were one way of communicating to a world without radio, television or Internet.] There were other 'souvenirs' offered for sale including: 'The Halifax Catastrophe Forty Views of Ruins. An attractive bound book of forty views showing extent of damage. Especially desirable for mailing to distant friends and Canadian soldiers overseas. Price mailed to any address 30 cents. On sale Marshall News Stores Halifax.'

Relief committees sent out 'thank you' letters or notes for publication in the newspapers, this one in answer to a request for an article in the *Yale News*:

'To: Harvey P. Clark, Esq., February 11, 1918, Care Yale News, New Haven, Conn.

…Express to you and through you to all those associated with you in the splendid contribution of clothing for the aid of the sufferers here our very sincere thanks for their thoughtful and tangible expression of sympathy….

… our neighbours in the great nation to the South performing magnificent service by rushing doctors, nurses, surgical supplies, food, clothing and money to our assistance as fast as trains, steamships and wire could be pressed into service.

The great commonwealth of Massachusetts is deserving of particular mention in the regard, since by Sunday, December 9, they had landed in Halifax a special train bringing nurses, doctors and hospital equipment galore. Ralph P. Bell, Secretary Relief Commission'

A flurry of letters occurred wanting to know various effects of the disaster. In this case the President of Dalhousie wrote to Captain Pascoe:

'February 20, 1918

Professor Bronson, of the University, and myself have been asked by the Royal Society of Canada to act as a Committee for the collection of observations of a scientific nature about the explosion of December 6th. …appreciate very highly any observations of your own on the nature of the air pressure or the water wave, or any other scientific data that would be of interest to the Royal Society.'

The reply:

'Naval Office, St. John, N.B.,
February 23rd, 1918.
A. Stanley MacKenzie, Esq.
President Dalhousie University,
Halifax, N. S.
Dear Sir:

… your request regarding information of the explosion.

I regret my barograph record was destroyed. I also regret that at the time of the explosion, I was in Captain Martin's house, knocked over, and more less dazed for a short period of time, and therefore, am unable to offer any observations that would be of any value.

Yours faithfully,
Captain Pascoe'

Prof. Howard Bronson of the Physics Department presented some 'Notes on the Halifax Explosion' to the Royal Society of Canada at its May 1918 meeting.

In the early part of 1918 awards were given for actions in Halifax on Dec. 6, 1917; many awards would be given posthumously such as the following example:

'Admiralty, 23rd March, 1918

The KING has been graciously pleased to approve the posthumous award of the Albert Medal in gold for gallantry in saving life at sea to:

Lieutenant-Commander (acting Commander) Tom Kenneth Triggs, R.N., and of the Albert Medal for gallantry in saving life at sea to:

Able Seaman William Becker, O.N.J. 5841

Of the seven people in the whaler, one Able Seaman Becker, was rescued alive on the Dartmouth shore, whither he had swum; the remainder perished.

It is clear…. Commander Triggs and the rest of the boat's crew were fully aware of the desperate nature of the work they were engaged in, and that by their devotion to duty they sacrificed their lives in the endeavour to save the lives of others.'

Spring must have been a welcome relief after months of living in cramped quarters, full of coal fumes, and the dim light of oil lamps. Rationing of supplies would continue for some items but the re-open-

Window of Halifax Hotel. The Reconstruction Office staff were busy for years rebuilding and repairing Halifax.

This house on Young St. facing Needham St. is the closest surviving structure to the explosion site. The sign in the photograph has often misled people into thinking it was newly built in 1918.

'—A Policemen—Handy Man [Newspaper 1918]
Police Officer James Eisenhower who has been on the force for over ten years is a carpenter and a glazer as well as a policeman. It is he who during the past weeks has made the City Hall habitable and his work attracted the attention of Colonel Bob Low. The colonel wants Eisenhower on his reconstruction gang and is willing to give him the opportunity to make from 4 to 6 dollars a day instead of the less than 2 dollars he makes as a police officer. Eisenhower is in a quandary. He does not like to lose the advantage of the time he has on the police force and at the same time the cost of present day living makes the construction offer attractive. Several of the newer men on the force have resigned for more lucrative employment.'

ing of the Public Gardens signalled a return of something familiar.

Slowly Halifax recovered and readied for a visit from, Governor Samuel McCall of Massachusetts, the man who had rallied his state to aid the stricken city. Correspondence of September 1918 requests that he stay longer so he might be properly thanked:

'J. J. Phelan, vice-Chairman, Massachusetts-Halifax Relief Committee, State House, Boston, Mass:

Governor McCall has wired that he will be in Halifax Sunday. Will you get in touch with him and urge him to stay over at least until Tuesday night so we may arrange a luncheon under the auspices of all business organizations here to testify how deeply we appreciate all that Massachusetts had done of us.

Mr. G. Fred Pearson, Chairman of Halifax Relief Committee'

The visit had to be postponed due to the outbreak of Influenza, known as Spanish Flu or Flanders Grippe, that became epidemic across North America. Many in Halifax were recovering from their injuries from the explosion of 1917 when they were taken ill with the flu. Some did not survive. Thousands would also die in Massachusetts. Nova Scotia would send nurses and doctors across the border to assist the state that had helped Halifax thus receiving the thanks of the Governor McCall. All public functions were cancelled and the

His Excellency Governor Samuel W. McCall of the Commonwealth of Massachusetts rallied the people of his state to the relief of the stricken people of Halifax.

Governor's trip to Halifax was delayed until November.
From *The Dalhousie Gazette* November 17, 1918:
'GOVERNOR OF MASSACHUSETTS VISITS DALHOUSIE
One of the most noteworthy events in the history of Dalhousie took place on Friday, November 10th, when a special convocation was held for the purpose of welcoming Governor Samuel McCall, fairy godfather of stricken Halifax, and tendering him thanks for the services rendered by him and his state, and also to inaugurate the Dennis Foundation chair of Government and Political Science.

The library was crowded to the doors with students and the most representative gathering of citizens ever convened at a college function. On the platform, in addition to the guest of honour, the faculty, the board of governors, the judges of Nova Scotia, and several others were Mrs. William Dennis and her daughter. Mrs. Dennis, with her husband, Senator Dennis, generously endowed the new chair in honour of their eldest son, Lieut. Eric Dennis, who died so gallantly in action. [Vimy Ridge Apr. 5, 1917]

An honourary degree of LL.D. was conferred upon Governor McCall in recognition of the prompt, voluntary, and inestimable aid sent to Halifax in the very first hours of her adversity last December. Before the degree was conferred, Professor Howard Murray read a particularly brilliant address, which, in polished style, embellished with pertinent classical allusions and clever bits of wit, sketched the Governor's career, as a student, lawyer, author, and statesman. It was quite the most effective event of the whole afternoon, and a far cry from the moments of agony spent in Latin One.

Governor McCall delivered the first lecture "Good Citizenship" in the Dennis Foundation. It was not so much a lecture as an informal talk delivered with infi-nite finish, eloquence, and charm, and, although it did not touch very closely upon political science, made the occasion one of pure delight to lovers of fine speaking. The reception tendered Governor McCall was hearty enough to show him that he has won from Dalhousie as well as from the grateful people of Halifax, an enduring affection.'

Governor McCall predicted to Halifax newspapers that he hoped word on the war ending 'would be heard in the next 72 hours.'

**The treasurer's statement of funds raised by the people of Massachusetts for the relief of Halifax. This account does not include donations of clothing, food and services. The remainder of the account was spent on medical care for survivors.**

| MASSACHUSETTS HALIFAX RELIEF FUND, JULY 1, 1919 | | |
|---|---|---|
| *Treasurer's Statement* | | |
| Total subscriptions, | $699,189 91 | |
| Rebates on bills, | 192 36 | |
| Interest on deposit, | 17,095 35 | |
| Total receipts, | | $716,477 62 |
| Expenditures for: — | | |
| Clothing, | $32,214 55 | |
| Material, | 23,167 36 | |
| Furniture, | 261,702 29 | |
| Supplies, | 40,369 64 | |
| Other essentials, | 95,164 95 | |
| Total expenditures, | | 452,618 79 |
| Balance on hand, | | $263,858 83 |
| On deposit as follows: — | | |
| Shawmut Bank, | | $161,180 84 |
| United States Trust Company, | | 102,677 99 |
| | | $263,858 83 |

GOV.MCCALL. APARTMENTS. EXPO. GROUNDS. OCT.9/18.

Temporary housing on the Exhibition Grounds, Almon Street
was toured by Governor McCall during his visit to Halifax.

Return of the Royal Canadian Regiment, one of many such
scenes of welcome for returning service personnel on the
Halifax waterfront throughout 1919.

# Chapter 12

# HALIFAX AFTER WORLD WAR I

*'The 88 Hydrostone buildings under construction or being erected by the Richmond Construction Company, Craig Building, Barrington Street, will afford safer and more fire-proof housing. The buildings will contain accommodation for 326 families and will be one of the largest and most modern developments ever constructed in Canada.'*

From a Nova Scotia Construction Company advertisement 1920s.

Firemen's arch erected as part of a welcoming parade on Barrington Street in 1919.

Shortly after Governor McCall's visit, at the 11th hour of the 11th day of the 11th month, World War I formally ended. For the next year returning personnel thronged Halifax, somewhat dazed on seeing the condition of the city they had left.

Across the world people had to adjust to their losses, so too Halifax. Dr. Victor Heiser of the Rockefeller Foundation, New York City advised setting up permanent health clinics. So beginning in 1919 for five years, $50,000 a year of Massachusetts Relief Fund money was voted for this purpose to ensure survivors received proper medical care.

The Relief Commission expropriated land in the Northend and created a development that became known as the Hydrostone. The name derived from the concrete blocks used in the construction of the buildings. Massachusetts' money bought furniture for the homes.

The Royal Family continued their interest in the Halifax relief effort. The highlight of that interest was the visit of Edward, Prince of Wales, August 19, 1919.

He laid cornerstones at the Town Clock, the Naval Building and Dalhousie University. He also spent time visiting the devastated Northend, meeting families and viewing reconstruction sites.

A Halifax newspaper reported: 'His Royal Highness visited for a half hour a newly finished house at 14 Cabot Place. He was reported to have studied the plan with "interest" and inspected the house "from top to bottom running down the stairs." The home visited was of a family where on Dec. 6, 1917 the father was at sea in Navy, the mother was crippled and disfigured, 2 sons, 5 & 7 died, a daughter survived.'

His Royal Highness, Edward, the Prince of Wales (right)
with the Lieutenant Governor of Nova Scotia, the
Honourable F. MacCallum Grant (left) and other dignitaries
on the steps of the Waegwoltic Club, Halifax, August 1919.
The Prince of Wales had high praise for the courage of the
people of Halifax.

## Significant events since 1919:

In the early 1920s businesses opened in the commercial block of the Hydrostone District.

March 22, 1920—Privy Council, the last Court of Appeal, gave the decision of Viscount Haldane, Lord Dunedin and Lord Atkinson regarding the collision in Halifax Harbour. The verdict stated both *Imo* and *Mont Blanc* at fault. The Captain of the *Imo*, Haakon Fron and the Pilot Hayes had been killed on December 6. The Captain of the *Mont Blanc*, Aimee LeMedec and the Pilot MacKay continued in their professions. Over the years it has been put forward that the curves in the harbour stream, the busy traffic, the sun and the actions of the ships' captains were all factors that contributed to cause the collision.

1920—Saint Joseph's basement church opens. Church finally completed in 1961. The parishioners rehouse their priests in a beautiful rectory as thanks for strength shown in days of turmoil.

July 16, 1920—cornerstone is laid for new Saint Mark's Church on Gottingen Street. First service February 1921.

1920—Rotary Club donates $3,000 for playground equipment in rebuilt area.

February 19, 1921—first permanent dial telephone exchange in Nova Scotia opened in Northend Halifax.

Construction and repairs of homes, churches, schools and businesses created a short economic boom in Nova Scotia but the returning military added to the work force and some people had to seek work elsewhere, especially in the Boston States.

1921—Saint Joseph's Convent—as the cornerstone was laid containing mementos of the disaster, the Sisters of Charity declared that the building was a sacred trust and bond with members of the parish. 'The new convent would not only provide a home for the Sisters but would also provide meeting places for various sodalities, a centre for lay retreats and work rooms for charitable projects for young and old.' The memorial to the women of the Children of Mary who died in the

The Hydrostone commercial block in Richmond District.

explosion was a tower bell. A parish bulletin reported: 'A few months following a retreat of the Children of Mary came the horror of the December 1917 disaster, taking from their midst eighteen of the Senior Sodality members and fourteen of the Juniors. Also, fourteen of the members were left widows, forty-nine families lost one or more members, fifty-nine members were badly injured and the homes of sixty-nine members were utterly destroyed.'

Cast upon the bell surface, in raised letters of bronze, is the name 'Ave Maria' and the names of the thirty-two members who perished:

Mrs. Frances Cash, Miss Kathleen Chisholm, Mrs. James Elliott, Miss Mary Elliott, Miss Stella Crawley, Mrs. Robert Ellis, Mrs. John Farrell, Miss Mary Flavin, Mrs. John Flavin, Miss Annie Jackson, Mrs. Elizabeth Flinn, Miss Susie Mooney, [she walked Walter Murphy Jr. to his first day of school], Mrs. James Jackson, Miss Florence Murray, Mrs. Joseph Langwith, Miss Margaret Purcell, Mrs. Frances McGill, Miss Mary Purcell, Mrs. Martin Murphy, [and her sister in law], Mrs. Patrick Murphy, Miss Mary Shea, Miss Aileen Stokes, Mrs. Charles O'Grady, Miss Bernadette Thomas, Mrs. Mary Pendergast, Miss Edna Walsh, Miss Mary Walsh, Mrs. Maurice Shea, Mrs. Thomas Shea, Mrs. Vincent Shea, Mrs. James Stockall, Miss Florence Young. [The bell is now in the museum at Mount Saint Vincent Motherhouse.]

September 18, 1921—United Memorial Church on Young Street dedicated, formed from the surviving members of the congregations of Kaye Street Methodist and Grove Presbyterian.

December 3, 1921—The *Imo* which had been refloated and rechristened *Gurernoren* as a whale oil tanker struck a rock off the Falkland Islands and was lost 3 days short of the 4th anniversary of the Halifax explosion.

1939—World War II, Halifax resumes its role as principal North American convoy port for allied nations.

1941—'Barometer Rising' a work of fiction by Hugh MacLennan, who was a witness to the explosion events from his home on South Park Street, is released and becomes a best seller.

1945—Atomic bombs dropped on Japan and World War II ends.

October 24, 1966—Halifax North Library opens on Gottingen Street dedicated to the victims of 1917. Sculpture on front lawn, is of fused metal depicting the city destroyed, rising again.

### Victoria General Pays Debt in 1961:

On December 6, 1917, Boy Scouts undertook all types of relief work. As messengers they ran notes around a city lacking telephone wires. The Chalobie Group rushed their first aid kit to the Victoria General Hospital where for a few minutes it filled a serious gap in supplies. The younger boys then set to work putting up materials to cover damaged windows. The older ones became orderlies, elevator operators, operating room attendants and days later guides on trucks for outside drivers who were unfamiliar with the streets of Halifax.

In December 1961 Hospital Administrator Dr. C. Bethune presented the 3rd Halifax Boy Scout troop with a replacement metal first aid cabinet as repayment of a 'Debt of Honour.'

Wreath laying at Fairview Lawn Cemetery in 1920s at the burial site of the unidentified dead from the 1917 Halifax explosion.

A view from Fort Needam of Hydrostone housing, 1920s. 'The 88 Hydrostone buildings under construction or being erected by the Richmond Construction Company, Craig Building, Barrington Street, will afford safer and more fire-proof housing. The buildings will contain accommodation for 326 families and will be one of the largest and most modern developments ever constructed in Canada.'

## The valiant efforts of the fire department:

Almost every day the Fire Department responded to coal embers that ignited along the rail lines to the docks. The Dec. 6 call of a fire at the Richmond Piers brought fireman from the West Street Fire Station. The explosion killed:

Fire Chief Edward P. Condon, Deputy Chief William P. Brunt, Captain William T. Broderick, Captain Michael Maltus, Hoseman John Spruin Sr., Hoseman John Duggan, Hoseman Walter Hennessey, Hoseman Frank Leary, Hoseman Frank Killeen.

The lone survivor on the fire truck 'Patricia' was driver Billy Wells. He was blown by the force of the explosion a distance away from the Patricia. His clothes were torn off as well

as the muscles from his right arm. The tidal wave washed over the pier sweeping away many bodies. He made his way along Campbell Road where the dead were hanging out windows or on overhead telegraph wires. He lay two days on the floor of Camp Hill Hospital waiting for a bed.

Billy Wells was presented with
**William [Billy] Wells.** part of the wheel from the 'Patricia.' He became a special constable and looked after the crosswalk by rebuilt Saint Joseph's School. He was known to give lunch money to children, retired in 1960 and died in 1971. His family returned the wheel to the Fire Department.

1976—Halifax Relief Commission closes operations and turns the remaining money over to the federal government to continue distribution as pensions for those severely injured or blinded by the blast.

June 9, 1985—Memorial Bell Tower, Fort Needham hill, Gottingen Street dedicated. Contains bells from United Memorial Church donated by Barbara Orr in memory of her mother, father, 5 brothers and sisters, all her immediate family and other relatives killed in 1917.

1987—Saint Joseph's Church unveils 9 windows depicting the story of the history of the parish including explosion and rebuilding.

1992—75th Anniversary Conference on the Disaster. Fireman's Memorial unveiled on Lady Hammond Road.

1997— 80th Anniversary of 'Great Disaster.'

1999— City Hall tower clock destroyed in explosion replaced.

## Conclusion:

Often when telling the story of the explosion to a group, many express surprise that they have never heard of it. For some it is a statistic in knowledge books listing disasters or explosions. Few know it was studied by those who developed the atomic bomb to understand the force of the blast, or that the collision was used as an example to show US naval personnel what not to do with a ship in similar circumstances. The disaster is not as easily recalled as the wartime sinking of the *Lusitania*. The individuals who assisted at Halifax, while making their mark in later life, are not as well remembered as others of the same time such as Lawrence of Arabia.

In 1917 Mr. Andrew Bonar Law stated to the British House of Commons of the explosion. 'It is a disaster which in peace time would have filled all our minds.' Indeed if the explosion had happened in peace time it might be more widely known around the world. However the story of the 1917 Halifax explosion was lost to the world in the upheaval following World War I—flu epidemics, the Depression and the Second World War.

In Halifax, December 6th is an honoured day of remembrance. Part of that is remembering the Americans who came unhesitatingly, worked tirelessly and gave money and supplies generously.

Since 1971 the Province of Nova Scotia has sent a Christmas tree to Boston as a token of appreciation for help given by the State of Massachusetts. The tree is erected at the Prudential Center.

Every year since 1985 a party is held on July 4 in Halifax to welcome American visitors on their national day and to recall the help given in 1917 by the people of the United States of America.

Locally the 1917 Halifax explosion will never be forgotten. It is remembered for the more than 2,000 dead. We remember it for the 387 doctors, the 30 members of the Canadian Army Dental Corps and the 760 nurses who aided the 9,000 seriously wounded. To be cherished is the kindness of the hundreds of volunteers whose work was only possible because of people from around the world who made donations of money and materials. It is an event that brought the best out in people who were complete strangers. It should always be remembered as a shining example of those who give aid to others in times of disaster.

The people housed in the temporary McCall apartments on the Exhibition Grounds would eventually move to the Hydrostone district or freestanding wooden houses in the Northend.

For many years only grave markers, such as the one dedicated to unidentified Catholic dead at Mount Olivet Cemetery (left), and memorial plaques marked the 1917 Halifax explosion. In the 1980s the need to rehouse bells from the United Memorial Church inspired the design for the Memorial Bell Tower (right) on Fort Needham.

# Selected Bibliography

*Barometer Rising,* School Edition, by Hugh MacLennan. Toronto: The MacMillian Company of Canada Limited at St. Martin's House, 1948.

*Bicentennial of the Halifax Fire Department: 1768-1968: 200 years of fire-fighting,* prepared by Pearl Connelly. Halifax: McCurdy Print, 1968.

*Catastrophe and social change, based upon a sociological study of the Halifax disaster,* by Samuel Henry Prince. New York: N.p., 1920.

*Death in Halifax,* by Edmund Gilligan. (Excerpt from *Reader's Digest,* condensed from *The American Mercury,* February, 1938).

*Grim visions: Arthur Lismer and the Halifax Explosion,* by Alan Ruffman. Halifax: Mount Saint Vincent University Art Gallery, 1990.

*Halifax catastrophe: forty views.* Halifax: Royal Print and Litho, 1917.

*Ground Zero, A Reassessment of the 1917 Halifax Explosion in Halifax Harbour,* Co-edited by Alan Ruffman and Colin D. Howell. Halifax: Co-published by Nimbus Publishing Limited and Goresbrook Institute for Atlantic Canada Studies at Saint Mary's University, 1994.

*Halifax disaster: December 6, 1917,* by Ernest Fraser Robinson. St. Catherine's, Ontario: Vanwell, 1987.

"Halifax explosion", by Thomas H. Raddall in *Atlantic anthology,* ed. by Will R. Bird. Toronto: McClelland and Stewart, 1959.

*Halifax explosion: December 6, 1917,* [compiled and edited] by Graham Metson. Toronto: McGraw-Hill, Ryerson, 1978.

*Halifax explosion: realities and myths,* by Alan Ruffman. Halifax: the author, 1987.

*Halifax relief expedition, December 6-15, 1917: report by Honourable A.C. Ratshesky, commissioner-in-charge, to Samuel Walker McCall, Governor of the Commonwealth of Massachusetts,* by A.C. Ratshesky. N.p.: Wright and Potter, 1918.

*Hugh MacLennan: a writer's life,* by Elspeth Cameron. Toronto: University of Toronto Press, 1981.

*In my time: a memoir,* by Thomas H. Raddall. Toronto: McClelland and Stewart, 1976.

*Name for himself: a biography of Thomas Head Raddall,* by Joyce Barkhouse. Toronto: Irwin, 1986.

*Naval service of Canada: its official history. Vol. 1: Origins and early years,* by Gilbert Norman Tucker. Ottawa: King's Printer, 1952.

*1917 Halifax explosion: 50th anniversary.* Halifax: N.p., 1967.

*"Portrait of a city",* by Hugh MacLennan in Atlantic Anthology, ed. by Will R. Bird. Toronto: McClelland and Stewart, 1959.

*Romance of the Halifax disaster,* by F. McKelvey Bell. Halifax: Royal Print and Litho, 1918.

*17 minutes to live,* by Richard A. Boning. Baldwin, N.Y.: Dexter & Westbrook, 1973.

*Town that died,* by Michael J. Bird. Toronto: McGraw-Hill, 1962.

*Views of the Halifax disaster, December 6,1917.* Halifax: N.p., 1917.

Public Archives of Nova Scotia
Halifax Explosion Collection MG 27
Halifax Relief Commission MG 36

Massachusetts State Archives
Massachusetts Halifax Relief, Committee files